Why Women Need
CHOCOLATE

Also by Debra Waterhouse, MPH, RD

Outsmarting the Female Fat Cell:
The First Weight-Control Program Designed
Specifically for Women

Why Women Need CHOCOLATE

Eat What You Crave to Look Good & Feel Great

BY

DEBRA WATERHOUSE, MPH, RD

NEW YORK

The programs in this book are not intended for persons with chronic ill-nesses or other conditions that may be worsened by an unsupervised eating program. The recommendations are not intended to replace or conflict with advice given to you by your physician or other health-care profession-als, and we recommend that you do consult your physician.

Library of Congress Cataloging-In-Publication Data

Waterhouse, Debra.
    Why women need chocolate : eat what you crave to look and feel
great / by Debra Waterhouse. — 1st ed.
        p.   cm.
    Includes bibliographical references.
    ISBN 0-7868-6051-0
    1. Women—Nutrition—Psychological aspects.   2. Mood
(Psychology)   3. Food habits.   4. Food preferences.   I. Title.
RA778.W219 1995
613.2'082—dc20   94-14966
                                                                              CIP

Design by ROBERT BULL DESIGN

FIRST EDITION

10   9   8   7   6   5   4   3   2   1

To my husband
Paul
whom I admire, respect, appreciate . . .
and love
even more than chocolate

ACKNOWLEDGMENTS

I CONSIDER MYSELF a very fortunate author. Surrounding me is a group of gifted and compassionate people who are my skilled advisers, enthusiastic coaches, and infinite supporters. These invaluable people are, not coincidentally, the same team that made my first book such a worthwhile and successful endeavor.

First and most important, my editor, Judith Riven, deserves far more than a simple acknowledgment. I never had to ask; she always anticipated my needs and eagerly offered her support, encouragement, expertise, and thoughtful insight— every day. She is a dear friend, an extraordinary editor, and an exceptional woman.

Bob Miller, my publisher, along with Brian DeFiore and the entire Hyperion crew, have shown unmatched dedication, belief, and commitment. A good manuscript only becomes a great book when the publishing company takes a sincere per-

•

sonal interest and goes beyond the call of duty. Hyperion is every author's dream come true.

A million thanks go to my fabulous literary agent, Sandra Dijkstra, whose brilliance in proposal development, contract negotiation, and foreign marketing never ceases to amaze me. I am truly blessed to have her representing me.

My lecture agent, Karen McElhatton of TalkPro in San Francisco, has been one of my most loyal supporters. Her great talent in promotion, public relations, and arranging speaking engagements has significantly advanced my career.

My sister, Lori Waterhouse Erwin, the mother of my three adorable nephews, often read chapters within the hour, always knew when to give praise, and more important, when to offer criticism. Her loving involvement in my writing and lecturing is priceless. I can never thank her enough.

My parents, Alina and Ray Waterhouse, have provided me with a lifetime of encouragement and support. The more I mature, the more I appreciate all they have done and continue to do.

A number of friends and colleagues came to my immediate aid with female wisdom, creative input, and speedy manuscript reading. My deepest appreciation goes to my sister-in-law Laura Euphrat, my friends Stephanie Goulding and Mary Pat Cedarleaf—and my friends *and* colleagues: Dr. Elizabeth Markley Holms, RD, Joyce Gertler, Ann Nicholson, and my co-worker of over ten years, Dr. Dee Tivenan.

And last, I would like to thank the thousands of women who have attended my seminars over the years. Their quest for knowledge and embrace of my philosophies have been inspirational!

•

CONTENTS

INTRODUCTION:
WOMEN NEED *WHAT*?!   3

CHAPTER ONE
EVE'S BLESSING: FEMALE FOOD CRAVINGS   13
Why Women?   15
Why Chocolate?   19
PMS: Positive Mood Swings   23
Menopause: Empowering the Mind   27
If Women Need Chocolate, What Do Men Need?   31
Eve's Blessing   32

CHAPTER TWO
SOCIETY'S EATING RULES LEAD TO FEMALE BLUES   34
The Mislabeled "Forbidden" Foods   36
Abstinence Makes the Craving Grow Stronger   41
Dieting and Brain Turbulence   42

The Balanced Meal Approach Does Not Balance
a Woman's Mood   43
For Women Only: The New, Improved Healthy Eating Rules   45

CHAPTER THREE
THE **ON** PLAN: **O**PTIMAL **N**UTRITION FOR MIND
AND BODY   48
The Principles of Pleasure Eating   51
The Five Steps to **O**ptimal **N**utrition for Mind and Body   53
Will This Plan Help Me Lose Weight?   57
Are You Ready for the **ON** Plan?   59

CHAPTER FOUR
STEP 1: TRUST YOUR FEMALE FOOD CRAVINGS   66
Once You Start Eating, You *Can* Stop   67
You Will *Not* Gain Weight   72
Your Diet Will *Not* Be Unhealthy   75
You *Can* Identify a Biological Food Craving   81
Week 1: Your **ON** Action Plan   87

CHAPTER FIVE
STEP 2: DISCOVER YOUR FEMALE PLEASURE FOODS   91
Starch: Your Brain's Longtime Companion   92
Sugar: A Bittersweet Relationship   99
Fat: The Friend That Wouldn't Leave   104
Chocolate: Optimal Brain Happiness   109
Protein: An Occasional Comrade   113
Salt: Your Premenstrual Pal   116
Week 2: Your **ON** Action Plan   122

CHAPTER SIX
STEP 3: LEARN HOW TO EAT FOR MAXIMUM
SATISFACTION   126
The Secrets of Taste Bud Satisfaction   127
The Secrets of Stomach Satisfaction   132

•

Substitutes Don't Satisfy   135
Gaining the Competitive Food-Mood Edge   137
Overeating Overloads the Brain   140
Week 3: Your **ON** Action Plan   143

CHAPTER SEVEN
STEP 4: DISTRIBUTE YOUR FOOD TO MAXIMIZE
MOOD   147
Five Small Meals for Big Benefits   149
Stabilizing the Destabilizers   155
10 to 4: The Hours to Say "Yes" to Food Cravings   161
The Not-So-Important Dinner   162
Week 4: Your **ON** Action Plan   168

CHAPTER EIGHT
STEP 5: FOLLOW YOUR OPTIMAL EATING ROUTINE   172
Optimal Eating for Your Daily Rhythms   174
Using Food to Your Rhythmic Advantage: Monthly and Yearly   184
When Your Brain Is under Strain   190
Week 5: Your **ON** Plan Evaluation   199

CHAPTER NINE
THE **ON** EXERCISE PLAN: YOUR FORMULA
FOR FEMALE FITNESS   206
Exercise, Endorphins, and LSD   210
The Female Fitness Formula for Fat-Burning   215
Fat-Burning Exercise Guidelines for Women   217
Overcoming Exercise Anxiety   222
The Woman's Workout: Designing Your Program   224

CHAPTER TEN
EMPOWERMENT EATING FOR A LIFETIME
OF WELL-BEING   227
Feel Good Today, Stay Healthy Tomorrow   228
Boning Up on Osteoporosis   231

•

xi

Getting to the Heart of Breast Cancer   236
Beyond Chocolate: Other Mood Enhancers   244
Food for All Your Needs: Brain, Body, Breasts, and Bones   245
Eve's Blessing   248

SUPPLEMENTS TO THE **ON** PLAN   249

GLOSSARY   251

REFERENCES   257

INDEX   267

•

Why Women Need
CHOCOLATE

Introduction:

I N ALL THE WORK I DO—counseling clients, conducting seminars, and writing books—I am committed to sharing honest and comforting messages with women. My first book, *Outsmarting the Female Fat Cell*, encouraged women to accept their fat-storing bodies, forgo dieting, the scale, and society's ideals—and work instead with the realities of a woman's body. From my initial and continued efforts with women to achieve a natural and comfortable weight, the birth of a new, powerful message has emerged: Women must also listen to their bodies and understand that the body's chemistry leads them to crave foods. If we are to enhance our well-being and successfully lose weight, we must learn to work with our female biologies *and* food cravings.

I believe that motivation comes from understanding. If you understand the way your female body functions, it will empower you to take care of yourself and respond to your

•

body's food needs every day—even when your body is telling you that it needs chocolate.

Yes, chocolate.

Not long ago, one of my clients, Susan, marched into my office with a look of frustrated defeat and declared, "I've been trying to fight a chocolate craving for over six hours, and I can't take it any longer. I've eaten lunch and a couple of snacks, but now I'm irritable, depressed, and my entire being is consumed with thoughts of chocolate. I need help!"

When I calmly responded, "Well, you could easily help yourself by fulfilling the craving and then experiencing the benefits of balanced moods and increased energy. Chocolate cravings are perfectly natural, and sometimes women need chocolate," she replied with shock and disbelief, **"Women need *what*?!** I've heard women need calcium for strong bones and iron for healthy blood, but I've only fantasized about women needing chocolate."

Well, you, just like Susan, can now stop fantasizing. Women *do* need chocolate as well as other foods high in starch, sugar, and fat to stabilize moods, control weight, and revitalize well-being. **Food cravings are Mother Nature's way of informing us that we need to eat a specific food in order to look and feel great!**

I'm sure that after reading the last paragraph, you now want a scientific explanation for why women need chocolate and how the fulfillment of food cravings can possibly lead to weight control and mood enhancement. I will share all there is to know about female food cravings so that you will gain an appreciation of the delicate balance of the female body, learn how to trust and benefit from its food messages, and finally understand many of the mysteries surrounding a woman's body (which after reading this book will not appear so mysterious at all):

•

- why 97% of all women surveyed report food cravings
- why the #1 food craved by women is chocolate
- why food cravings intensify during and after a diet
- why denial and restriction lead to weight gain
- why food cravings intensify premenstrually and during the transition of menopause
- why women have the strongest food cravings in the late afternoon and early evening
- why sleep difficulties are 3 times more common in women
- why seasonal depression is 6 times more common in women
- why women are more sensitive to blood sugar changes and, therefore, need to eat more frequently throughout the day
- why women can't successfully follow a very low-fat and low-sugar diet

So, why women?

Women are wonderfully unique, ever-changing, compassionate beings. We have estrogen. We have mood swings. We have food cravings. We have special food needs. We did 1,000 years ago, 100 years ago, and we do today. Each of these physical and emotional traits is an integral part of being a woman—and their balance is vital to a woman's mind and body.

Recently, a new field of nutrition and women's health has emerged: the study of the effects of estrogen and food on powerful mood-modifying brain chemicals. My first chapter will provide a full and uncomplicated explanation, but for starters here are some research highlights:

Over a decade ago, scientists at the Massachusetts Institute of Technology began the search for a link between food and mood. They found that various foods high in sugar and starch boosted a potent brain chemical called serotonin that

•

brought about feelings of calmness and general mood stability. It wasn't until more recently, however, that the evidence surfaced relating the food-mood link specifically to women. Researchers at Rockefeller University in New York found that food cravings coincided perfectly with reproductive needs. Women frequently craved sugar because of estrogen's effect on brain chemicals and blood sugar levels. This effect explained why female food cravings emerged at puberty, intensified premenstrually and during pregnancy, and diminished (but didn't disappear) after menopause.

With the connection between women and sugar cravings on solid scientific ground, University of Michigan researchers took the female food-mood link one step further: Women didn't just crave sugar for its calming effects, they also craved fat for its mood-elevating effects. Fat was found to release another brain chemical, the endorphins, which energized the mind and lifted the spirit. Indeed, the most powerful female food cravings are for sugar *and* fat combinations—with the most powerful craving of all for, of course, chocolate. Chocolate has the perfect combination of sugar and fat, plus a plethora of other ingredients that account for its unmatched biological and psychological experience.

Wait! The research discoveries get even more interesting. Back at Rockefeller University and the Massachusetts Institute of Technology, researchers were busy trying to figure out what to do about these sugar/fat food cravings and found that the best way to manage food cravings is to satisfy them immediately with a small portion. Abstinence and restriction only served to fuel the food cravings, trigger binge eating, and further deteriorate mood—while fulfillment satisfied the craving, prevented overeating, and enhanced mood. The enlightening conclusion: **food cravings are not a problem to be treated, but a blessing to be encouraged.**

•

The scientific research explains why women crave chocolate, sugar, and fat—and the vital reasons why women should always respond to their food cravings. When we listen to our bodies and give ourselves guilt-free permission to immediately fulfill our food cravings, we will feel better, function more efficiently, eat less, control our weight—and we'll *never* have to diet again.

Marketing research, food consumption analysis, and statistical surveys are all arriving at the same conclusions on the gender differences in appetite: Women are more likely to buy and eat high sugar foods, fruits, and rich desserts while men are more likely to buy and eat meat, meat, and meat. Why is there such a strong bond between men and meat? Men biologically need more protein because they have more testosterone and greater muscle mass. In contrast, women biologically need more sugar and fat because we have more estrogen and more body fat.

In the course of my research for this book, I undertook an extensive food-craving survey with over 600 respondents. I will provide some of the results here, but will also integrate the information into appropriate chapters throughout the book. The results of my survey support all past research as well as uncover some new gender differences in food cravings and appetite.

The gender differences speak for themselves: **Women prefer, crave, and eat more chocolate, sugar, starch, and fat—and when we fulfill our food cravings, we feel better.**

Despite all the persuasive research supporting female food cravings and the gender differences in appetite, the study of food cravings and the effect of food on brain chemistry is in its infancy. Solid relationships have been identified, but there are still many unanswered questions. Like all educa-

•

WOMEN ARE ...	**MEN ARE ...**
76% more likely to crave chocolate	78% more likely to crave meat
71% more likely to crave crackers	76% more likely to crave eggs
62% more likely to crave ice cream	69% more likely to crave hot dogs
62% more likely to crave candy	10% more likely to crave pizza
65% more likely to crave fruit	10% more likely to crave seafood

Most Likely to Prefer:
#1 chocolate
#2 bread
#3 ice cream

Most Likely to Prefer:
#1 red meat
#2 pizza
#3 potatoes
(64% of the men left this part
of the survey blank!)

6 times more likely to "love" chocolate	5 times more likely to "dislike" chocolate
22 times more likely to eat chocolate to feel better	1½ times more likely to exercise to feel better
2 times more likely to feel good when they *fulfill* their food cravings	4 times more likely to feel good when they *deny* their food cravings
2 times more likely to binge on their craved foods	2 times more likely to follow a very low fat and sugar diet
2 times more likely to feel fatigued and depressed	2 times more likely to feel satisfied with artificial sweeteners and fake fats

tors, I have taken the current scientific facts and applied them to benefit my clients. The overwhelmingly positive results are here for you to take advantage of in the step-by-step approach of the "**ON** Plan: **O**ptimal **N**utrition for Mind and Body":

Step 1: Trust Your Female Food Cravings
Step 2: Discover Your Female Pleasure Foods
Step 3: Learn How to Eat for Maximum Satisfaction
Step 4: Distribute Your Food to Maximize Mood
Step 5: Follow Your Optimal Eating Routine

These five steps *are* the new, improved healthy eating guidelines for women. When you make a commitment to the **ON** Plan, and begin fulfilling your special female food needs, you will learn how to:

- honor your female body and respect your food cravings
- satisfy your food cravings *without* guilt, *without* overindulgence, and *without* weight gain
- achieve a comfortable, realistic weight by fulfilling your food cravings
- overcome your food-craving fears
- confidently differentiate between an emotional food craving and a biological food craving
- have more positive premenstrual and menopausal experiences
- experience maximum pleasure and satisfaction from food
- find the balance where food is providing both the immediate mood-energy benefits as well as the long-term health benefits
- discover an optimal eating routine that is best for your body, your mind, and your lifestyle

•

The **ON** Plan has proven to be successful with thousands of women, but what I am advocating in this book may at first appear inconsistent with the universally accepted principles of good nutrition. You may stop in mid-sentence and declare, "Wait a minute! Everything I read, hear, and watch tells me that fat is the culprit, sugar is white death, and chocolate is the most decadent food in the world. Won't I become obese and die of heart disease, cancer, and diabetes simultaneously?"

You may if you eat a lot of these foods all the time, but you won't if you trust your food cravings, immediately respond to them with small amounts, and use them to balance your brain chemistry and moods. As you will discover (perhaps some of you with some slight disappointment), biological food cravings can be satisfied with surprisingly small amounts of food. When you start to satisfy these urges, you'll find that the messages are subtle and completely manageable. Even more important, you'll be a happier person.

It's when you *don't* satisfy food cravings that they can become uncontrollable. With denial, our perceived need becomes a pound of chocolate instead of a piece, a bag of chips instead of a handful, a quart of ice cream instead of a scoop, or a loaf of bread instead of a slice. Then you will gain weight and increase your risk of disease.

The **ON** Plan is the solution to out-of-control eating behavior and weight struggles, but let me take a moment to tell you what the **ON** Plan isn't. It is *not* an excuse to eat chocolate morning, noon, and night. It is *not* the solution to emotional eating. Although I will help you to distinguish between an emotional and biological food craving, those women who frequently eat for emotional reasons must first come to terms with their underlying emotional triggers before they can benefit from this approach. The **ON** Plan is also *not* the answer to clinical depression, chronic fatigue syndrome, addictions,

•

Seasonal Affective Disorder, bulimia, or compulsive overeating. However, most women do not fall into the extremes. There are varying degrees of depression, fatigue, and distorted eating behavior—and the **ON** Plan approach *will* help you to establish a healthier relationship with your mind and body.

Throughout this book, I will be sharing comments, experiences, and anecdotes from many clients and seminar attendees. To conclude this introduction, let me share one client's experience with the **ON** Plan.

Susan, who at first asked unbelievingly, "Women need *what?!*" and provided the title for this introduction, also ultimately changed her life with the **ON** Plan. "I remember as a young girl my mother forbidding me to eat chocolate or anything with sugar for fear that I would gain weight and become overweight like her. At age twelve, I used to hide cookies underneath my bed and chocolate bars in the bushes outside. At age thirty-five, I was still hiding these foods from my husband and still binging on them when no one was home. Ridden with guilt, I'd try to go cold turkey every now and then, I'd drink a six-pack of diet soda a day to get my sweet fix, I even tried hypnosis once. But nothing worked. I was out of control, unhappy, irritable, moody, and I was taking it out on my husband, my kids, and my co-workers."

"I never thought that I could ever be at peace with food, my mind, and my body, but I feel like I am taking care of myself for the first time in my life. By following the **ON** Plan, I feel like a new person. I trust my cravings and respond to them right away. I don't need the package of cookies or the box of chocolate bars any longer; a couple of cookies or a piece of chocolate does the trick, and I can go about my day with renewed energy and vitality. And there's more: I've actually lost weight and regained the respect of my family and

•

peers. I know that this is right for my body because it feels too good not to be."

You, too, can experience all of the benefits of trusting and fulfilling your female food cravings. You can learn to enjoy complete satisfaction from food without guilt, without weight gain, and without losing control. You can achieve pleasure, fulfillment, a healthy body, and a happy mind—all at the same time!

Read on and learn how to follow your eating instincts and satisfy your food cravings. Let the natural ability of food maximize your mood, boost your energy level, and revitalize your well-being!

•

One

YOU ARE SITTING at your desk writing a letter when all of a sudden a food craving emerges. That craving may be for chocolate, candy, chicken, or Chinese food—but it's there, it's powerful, and it's asking for fulfillment.

From past experience, you know that if you try to ignore the craving, it will only intensify and preoccupy you, so instead you choose to stop what you are doing and satisfy it. When you sit back down at the desk, you are aware of some significant changes: The craving has disappeared, you feel better, and you have more energy and creativity to accomplish what has to get done.

You made a wise choice. You responded to a female food craving.

Certain food cravings are unique to our gender and emerge for vital purposes. They are messages from our bodies informing us that we need to eat a specific food in order to

•

feel and function better. When we listen to these important messages and respond to our food cravings, their fulfillment has the amazing ability to:

- lift our spirits when we are down
- boost our energy when we are fatigued
- fuel our bodies when we need nutrition
- calm our nerves when we are stressed
- stabilize our moods when we are premenstrual
- empower our minds when we are menopausal

But unfortunately, food craving fulfillment is seldom described with these beneficial qualities. The dictionary defines the word *craving* as "an abnormal desire." Abnormal? Not when it comes to women and food. Based on a woman's physiology, food cravings are perfectly normal and natural. They are based on real bio*logical* needs: what is *logical* for the body. When you biologically need something, you strive to fulfill that need. When you need to sleep, you go to bed. When you need to warm your body, you put on a sweater. When you need chocolate, you *should* eat it.

Maybe someday the dictionary will add a new entry:

Female Food Craving: a normal, biological need for a specific food that will balance a woman's body and mind and revitalize her well-being

It may sound too good to be true, but research across the world is proving that female food cravings are a blessing. They are messages that we can't and shouldn't ignore.

Food cravings are a natural part of being a woman.

•

WHY WOMEN?

We can thank our female sex hormone, estrogen, and our life-giving functions of pregnancy and breast-feeding for the inborn food wisdom that keeps us in such close communication with our body's needs. The appetite center is right next door to the reproductive center in our brains, and these neighbors strive to keep the female body healthy. This positioning is not coincidental; our food cravings make sure that we have enough fat on our bodies for fertility, that we have the proper nutrition for a healthy body, that we have stable blood sugar levels for sustained energy, and that we have balanced brain chemicals for stable moods.

What women biologically crave is a reflection of what the female body biologically needs.

- Sometimes we crave the specific foods that will enhance our nutritional status, such as oranges for their high vitamin C content.
- Sometimes we crave the specific foods that will enhance our blood sugar levels, such as bread or candy for their high carbohydrate content.
- And sometimes we crave the specific foods that will enhance our brain chemicals, such as fat, sugar, starch and, of course, chocolate for their remarkable effects on brain chemistry.

The brain chemistry–food craving relationship is a new, provocative area of research, and deserves a brief explanation in this first chapter. Don't worry, the biochemical explanation will be short and simple, with only the basics necessary to appreciate the way your female brain functions and how foods can positively affect brain chemicals and thus mood.

Through the messages of brain chemicals called neuro-

•

transmitters, your brain does a fabulous job of communicating exactly what it needs for optimal functioning. These brain chemicals "transmit" messages from one brain cell (neuron) to another. There are hundreds of neurotransmitters, but two appear to be most important for female brain cell communication, mood stability, and food cravings:

> **Serotonin** is a chemical released after eating carbohydrates that transmits calmness and mood stability to your brain cells
>
> **Endorphins** are chemicals released after eating fat and chocolate that transmit high-level energy and euphoria to your brain cells

Serotonin and the endorphins are your "feel good" brain chemicals, and carbohydrates, fats, and chocolate are your "feel good" foods. They all work together to help you look and feel your best. In Chapter 5, I will provide an in-depth explanation of how they join forces, but let me give you an example now to make them feel more reader-friendly.

When your brain cells' level of serotonin is low, they don't have the ability to send the "feel good" messages, and, therefore, you feel irritable and moody. You biologically crave starch (breads, pasta, potatoes) or sugar (candy, soft drinks, fruits, fruit juice) to boost serotonin and balance your moods. And, most important, when you respond to your cravings, the rewards are great. You feel calm and productive.

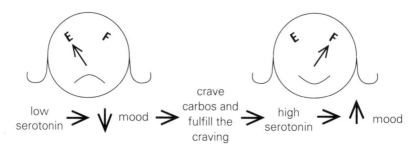

low serotonin → ⇓ mood → crave carbos and fulfill the craving → high serotonin → ⇑ mood

•

Endorphins work similarly to serotonin. When endorphin levels are low in your brain cells, you feel stressed and fatigued. You biologically crave fat or chocolate to boost endorphins; when you fulfill the cravings, you fill the "feel good" tank, and your spirits are lifted.

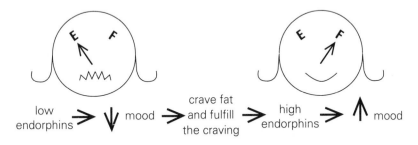

low endorphins ➤ ↓ mood ➤ crave fat and fulfill the craving ➤ high endorphins ➤ ↑ mood

It is quite possible for both of these brain chemicals to run empty simultaneously so that we crave sugar and fat together. Actually, it's more than possible. Research has found that women are more likely to crave sugar/fat combinations than sugar or fat alone. It should come as no surprise to hear that chocolate is the perfect combination of sugar and fat!

You may be wondering what would cause these brain chemicals to get out of balance in the first place. As the research on brain chemistry continues to increase, it seems as if almost anything can affect female brain chemistry: hormonal fluctuations, seasonal changes, eating habits, stress, and sleep deprivation. I will address all of these factors and more in the upcoming chapters. But whatever the cause of brain chemical changes, you now have the awareness that you can quickly bring your body and mind back into balance by responding to your food cravings.

Next, I want to give you an understanding of why women are born to be so biologically in tune with their food needs in the first place. Our need and desire for certain foods goes beyond mental and physical well-being to an even more pri-

•

mal need—survival. Just about everything has a biological basis, and the explanation for female food cravings goes back to the feast-and-famine cycles of yesterday.

Since women are responsible for the survival of the human race, the female body evolved so that it does whatever it possibly can to survive famines—to store fat efficiently, to release fat reluctantly, and to crave high-calorie foods so that we will have enough stored body fat to stay fertile and carry a developing child for nine months.

Our female food cravings most likely originated to encourage us to eat the highest-calorie foods available so that even in the midst of a famine, we would have the necessary calories to survive and to store. Thousands of years ago, the sweetest berries and fattiest animal meats were stimulating the release of the pleasurable brain chemicals, serotonin and the endorphins, and these chemicals made us feel so good that we wanted to search for the high-sugar/high-fat foods for energy and mood enhancement whenever we had the chance.

Today we are still searching, although now we don't have to look very far. We may no longer crave the sweetest berries or animal fats, but we do still crave high-fat and/or high-sugar foods: jelly beans, fruit, donuts, cakes, marshmallows, cookies, pies, ice cream, potato chips, cream puffs, and chocolate.

"So you're saying that women need chocolate for survival?" asked one of my clients, Abby. "Should I include a pound of chocolate in my earthquake survival kit?" (Living in California, we think about things like earthquake survival, and come to think of it, packing some chocolate may not be a bad idea.) Women need to store plenty of body fat for survival, and if a natural disaster were to occur, you would definitely be craving chocolate as your survival mechanism kicked into gear.

•

Let me summarize the biological basis of female food cravings. We crave specific foods because of:

1. our body's survival instinct—**store, store, store**
2. our female hormone, estrogen, and our special functions of pregnancy and breast-feeding
3. our blood sugar needs
4. our nutrient needs
5. our brain chemical needs with the food-mood connection

The forces that dictate our female food needs are biologically ingrained. That's why cravings cannot be controlled or fought with willpower—but they can be managed and experienced with the "will" to "power" our bodies and minds with the foods we were designed to eat.

And—as the title of this book emphasizes—chocolate appears to "power" the female body and mind more than any other food.

WHY CHOCOLATE?

The proof is in the (chocolate) pudding:

- 97% of all women surveyed report food cravings, 68% of which are for chocolate.
- 50% of all women surveyed say that they would choose chocolate over sex.
- women are 22 times more likely than men to choose chocolate as a mood enhancer.
- 3.4 million dollars are spent annually on chocolate, the majority of it out of women's wallets.

When survey after survey, paper after paper, study after study, find that a woman's number-one food craving is for

•

chocolate, followed by foods like ice cream, candy, and bread—there *must* be a reason. No study has ever found that women frequently crave tofu, Spam, or nonfat cottage cheese, and no study has ever found that men frequently crave chocolate or jelly beans. Only women crave these foods consistently.

What makes chocolate so special to a woman's brain and body?

Our efficient brain chemistry and survival mechanism account for much of the craving, but there is more to the anatomy of a chocolate craving. Taste, habit, emotional attachment, and cultural influences also define the foods we crave. **The psychological experience is as much involved as is the biological phenomenon.**

First let's address the biological phenomenon. Chocolate derives about 50 percent of its calories from sugar, so it boosts serotonin levels in the brain. It also derives about half of its calories from fat. At the same time, therefore, it can boost brain endorphin levels—and the result is powerful: All brain chemicals are positioned at optimal levels for positive moods and renewed energy.

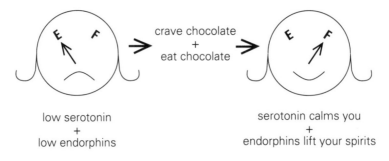

crave chocolate
+
eat chocolate

low serotonin
+
low endorphins

serotonin calms you
+
endorphins lift your spirits

You'd think that this positive effect on brain chemicals should be enough, but there is even more to the biological chocolate experience. Chocolate also contains other compounds that may have additional benefits for brain function:

•

- It contains phenylethylamine, a chemical released in our brain when we fall in love. Whether it's the exact same chemical or not is still under investigation, but the possibility that it is the same could explain why 50% of all women surveyed say they would choose chocolate over sex.
- It contains theobromine, a substance similar to caffeine that affects brain function in a positive way by increasing our alertness, concentration, and cognitive functioning.
- It contains magnesium, a mineral involved in manufacturing serotonin and stabilizing mood.

"That's right! I read somewhere that women crave chocolate because we are deficient in magnesium." When I explained to my chocolate-loving client, Kathryn, that she would need to eat about a dozen chocolate bars to get her daily recommended dose of magnesium, her quick response was, "No problem."

If your body were really craving magnesium, you'd go for something like spinach or Swiss chard. So it's probably not the magnesium alone, but perhaps a combination of all the physical elements of chocolate that elicits such a pleasurable biological response: sugar, fat, phenylethylamine, theobromine, and magnesium. Not to mention that chocolate comes from the Theobroma tree, which means "food of the gods."

Now for the metaphysical elements of chocolate that account for the psychological experience.

- It has a melting point of 97 degrees, just below body temperature, so it melts immediately and pleasures your taste buds in a way that no other food can.
- It has a blend of over 500 flavors (2½ times more than any other food), so its sensory properties are unmatched by any other food.

•

- It has been given as a reward since childhood when you cleaned your room or ate your veggies.
- It has had medicinal properties since childhood when we skinned our knee or felt sad.
- It continues to be the most frequently given gift to declare love, appreciation, and gratitude.

Some researchers feel that this psychological experience is primarily responsible for our love affair with chocolate. Others feel that it is mostly the biological phenomenon. I personally feel that the combination—the entire experience—creates the romance.

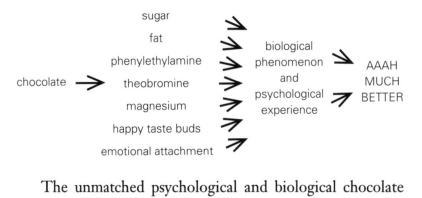

The unmatched psychological and biological chocolate experience has been acknowledged for centuries. The Aztecs discovered the cocoa bean and the pleasures of a chocolate beverage, but they forbade women to consume it because the drink was considered to be an aphrodisiac (probably the phenylethylamine!). However, women didn't stand for the chocolate restriction for long, and by the year 1518 chocolate was being enjoyed by the nobles of Spain and shortly thereafter made its way through Europe and beyond.

Some women don't crave chocolate, and they often ask me if something is wrong with their biochemistries. Abso-

•

lutely nothing is wrong. If it's not chocolate you crave, it's another food high in sugar and fat that will fulfill the same biological and psychological needs.

Whatever the foods you crave, we have discussed the reasons why you crave them and why you should listen to your body and respond to your special biological needs—every day. However, there are certain days when food cravings are strongest and warrant special attention: the few days before you start your period and the many, many days of the menopausal transition.

PMS: POSITIVE MOOD SWINGS

Over forty years ago, Dr. Katrina Dalton coined the term *PMS* (for Premenstrual Syndrome), and it has become one of the most common acronyms in our vocabulary. Unfortunately, it has also become a term with a negative connotation. A few days before we start our periods many of us are called irritable, bitchy, emotionally unstable, and irrational.

At times, these descriptions may have some accuracy (although greatly exaggerated), but I prefer to define PMS as Positive Mood Swings—standing for increased creativity and compassion instead of increased confusion and chaos. How so? **By fulfilling your food cravings and respecting your heightened emotions, you will bring your monthly rhythms and brain chemicals into balance.**

PMS is not a disorder. It's not a disease. It's not a psychological illness. It's a natural biological event that most women experience each and every month. Only the degree to which we experience it differs. Even if you experience magnified premenstrual symptoms every month, PMS can still stand for Positive Mood Swings, if you appreciate your mood changes and respond to your food cravings.

•

Joanne was a disbeliever. She couldn't imagine that her PMS could resemble anything positive. As she described it, "Life isn't one damn thing after another. It's the same damn thing over and over and over and over again." But the following explanation convinced Joanne that she could balance her premenstrual moods and energy levels.

The 150+ changes that women may experience premenstrually can be explained through hormonal fluctuations and brain chemistry changes. During your monthly cycle, estrogen and progesterone levels are changing, and this is what can happen to serotonin levels in your brain:

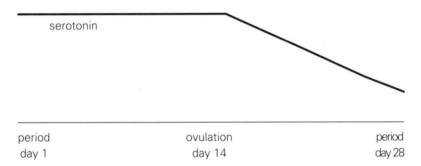

period	ovulation	period
day 1	day 14	day 28

After ovulation, during the last two weeks of your monthly cycle, the brain's serotonin level drops, causing a drop in mood and energy. Women crave sugar more often as a natural way to boost serotonin levels and produce calmness and mood stability. Because our serotonin levels are lowest a few days before our periods, our sugar cravings are the strongest then. By understanding these biological changes, anticipating them, and responding to your food cravings—you can boost your serotonin levels and achieve a more positive premenstrual experience.

•

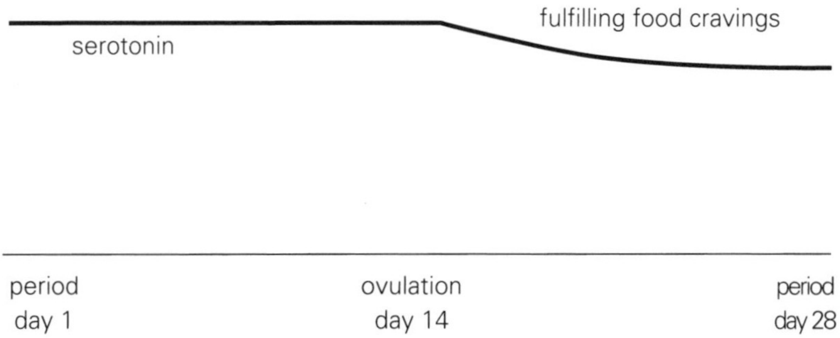

fulfilling food cravings

serotonin

| period | ovulation | period |
| day 1 | day 14 | day 28 |

Sugar is not the only food that women crave premenstrually. The number-one craved food is, not surprisingly, chocolate. We are more likely to crave chocolate candy instead of lollipops, and chocolate ice cream instead of orange Popsicles. Our bodies are directing us toward sugar and fat combinations—for brain serotonin *and* endorphin release.

At ovulation, something else is going on I'd like to tell you about. It's the "endorphin surge," a short time span of about forty-eight hours during which endorphin levels rise dramatically and then drop back down to normal levels. Over the last two weeks of your menstrual cycle, your body and brain are withdrawing from the high endorphins. It's like coming off a drug. As we are withdrawing from the endorphins, we become lethargic and anxious and we crave chocolate and other high-fat foods.

•

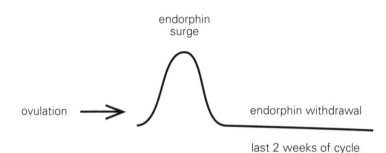

By satisfying your premenstrual chocolate cravings and boosting endorphin levels during the last two weeks of your menstrual cycle, you can ease the endorphin withdrawal and thus stabilize your moods.

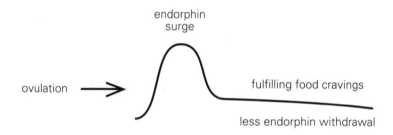

You may be wondering why the endorphin surge happens at all. Well, it has its reproductive purposes and probably originated so that conception would occur. Endorphins make you feel great, and since you are fertile for only forty-eight hours every month—let's do what we are supposed to do when we are fertile, and get that egg fertilized!

Yes, endorphins increase your sex drive. They also make your skin vibrant, your hair more manageable, and your mind more creative. Since childhood, I can remember my mother

•

telling me that women have two exceptional days a month. This insight was based on her own intuitive awareness, and her theory has now been proven with the discovery of the endorphin surge. According to my mother, during those forty-eight hours, you should schedule all social events, interviews, important meetings, and television appearances. When I first started my business, I tried to follow my mother's advice, but the stress this kind of scheduling produced negated any benefit from the endorphins.

"Now it all makes complete sense to me. Why after I start my period, I feel neutral, why at mid-cycle when I ovulate I feel great, and why before my period, I'm sensitive, emotional, and would sell my soul for chocolate." It also finally made sense to Samantha that she should always listen to her instinctive food needs and respond to her biological food cravings. They are the answer to having a more positive premenstrual experience.

MENOPAUSE: EMPOWERING THE MIND

Another time in our lives when we have an inborn food wisdom and increased food cravings is during the transition to menopause. Just like PMS, menopause is a natural biological event that *all* women experience, or as Karen said, "I've revised the old phrase that there are two things in life you can't avoid: taxes and death. There are three things in life women can't avoid: taxes, death—and menopause." Karen is also an example of a woman who never really craved chocolate until she began the transition to menopause, or, as it is called now, perimenopause—which, by the way, can last anywhere from six months to fifteen years.

Many factors influence the length and intensity of the menopausal experience and many biological changes occur in

•

a woman's body during this transition. Unfortunately, our society has traditionally viewed these changes as negative: loss of femininity, loss of youth, loss of sanity, and the "beginning of the end of life." These phrases do *not* accurately describe the menopausal experience, and I strongly feel that it is important to take a more positive approach. Most women are actually relieved that they no longer have their periods and no longer have to think about contraception. And about 20 percent of all women experience *positive* changes during menopause: increased energy, increased productivity, and an increased sex drive.

"Why can't I be one of those 20 percent? I have no energy and no interest in sex." As I explained to Karen, each woman's experience with perimenopause is different, and unfortunately, we are constantly made aware of the negative changes: the depression, the anxiety, the mood swings, the fatigue, the hot flashes, the weight gain, and the increased risk of disease.

And—let's not forget to mention forgetfulness. After a session together, Karen called me up a few hours later saying, "I forgot to tell you about my menopausal memory loss." We both laughed, but we also knew that the symptom is real and can affect a woman's life. Some memory loss is perfectly natural during perimenopause and as we grow older. If you forget where you put your car keys and frantically search the house, that's natural. If you stare at your car keys and forget what they are for, that's another situation entirely—and you should definitely report this to your physician.

During perimenopause, all of the changes in a woman's mind and body can be explained through the fluctuations in female sex hormones. Many of the mood changes may be due to a drop in brain serotonin caused by the decline in estrogen. This drop explains the intensified sugar cravings as the brain

•

tries to bring serotonin back up to normal levels. But what about the chocolate and fat cravings?

Let's go back to the endorphin surge at ovulation. A woman's body is trying to stay fertile during perimenopause and keep her eggs in production. As your body is trying to ovulate, the hormones that stimulate the egg release, follicle-stimulating hormone and luteinizing hormone, are produced at much higher levels. One explanation is that the higher these hormones, the higher the endorphin surge; the higher the endorphin surge, the greater the endorphin withdrawal—and the stronger the chocolate cravings.

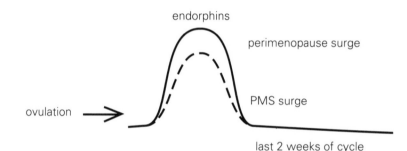

The changes that occur in a woman's body during menopause are natural and biologically understandable: the mood changes, the body changes, even the weight gain. The average weight gain is about twelve pounds, and it may not be ideal, but virtually all women gain some weight. If all women gain some weight during perimenopause, there must be a reason. Actually, there are two reasons.

1. **To provide a natural source of estrogen** As the ovaries stop producing estrogen, the fat cells take over and are the primary source of estrogen production for postmenopausal women. Mother Nature provided a means of naturally pro-

•

ducing estrogen, and gaining weight helps. Therefore, some of the extra body fat gained during menopause is necessary. Hormone-replacement therapy has been available for only forty years or so, but the ability of fat cells to produce estrogen has been around forever.

2. **To reduce the risk of osteoporosis** Carrying some additional weight is also beneficial for bone health. Risk of osteoporosis and bone fractures increases during and after menopause. The more body weight you have to carry around, the stronger your bones become in order to withstand that additional weight. That assumes, of course, that you move your body.

"So, the next time I go to the doctor's and get the your-weight-is-up-from-last-year look, I can stand up straight and boldly say that I gained weight on purpose to prevent osteoporosis?" Sure, you can say it, but your doctor probably won't buy it. Other options are available, such as weight-bearing exercises and a calcium-rich diet to strengthen bones.

For the perimenopausal woman, acting upon increased cravings for higher-calorie foods—such as chocolate, sugar, and fat—ensures some additional weight gain, balances the brain chemical changes, decreases the mood changes, and empowers the mind.

"Why don't men have these monthly cycles and the 'change of life'?" asked Jan. "Or do they?" Some research supports various monthly hormonal fluctuations in men, appropriately called PTS, or Pre-Testosterone Syndrome. Even more research is available to provide evidence for a type of male menopause where testosterone levels significantly decline between the ages of forty and sixty. During the male menopause, there may be some mood changes, but the most common symptom is a decline in virility, and even George

•

Burns has joked about how although everything that goes up must come down, for most men eventually everything that's down won't come up.

Speaking of men, do they have cravings for specific foods like we do?

IF WOMEN NEED CHOCOLATE, WHAT DO MEN NEED?

When I pose this question to my seminar groups, the women usually yell out with confidence, "Beer!" and the men respond more quietly, "Meat." I don't think beer is included in the food-craving surveys so I can't comment on the accuracy of that response, but meat and other protein foods are always included in the surveys—and that's universally what men seem to crave. But men don't usually call them food cravings; they call them "food preferences" because the desire and need is not as strong.

The foods most frequently craved/preferred by men are meat, hot dogs, and eggs—all protein foods. The foods most frequently craved by women are chocolate, ice cream, and bread. The sexes couldn't be more different.

Think of the men in your life:

- How often have you seen them go down to the store at midnight just to fulfill their craving for chocolate chocolate-chip ice cream?
- How often have you witnessed them binging on a package of cookies when their hormones are imbalanced and they've had a tough day?
- How often have you seen them curled up in their favorite chair experiencing the pleasure of slowing eating a chocolate truffle?

•

Probably not very often. But I bet you have seen them consuming steak and eggs for breakfast, hot dogs for lunch, and meat and potatoes for dinner.

The differences in sex hormones and body composition explain the differences in the foods men and women crave. You already know that women have larger amounts of estrogen, larger fat cells, and cravings for sugar and fat. Well, men have larger amounts of testosterone, smaller fat cells, and about forty pounds more muscle mass than we do. From puberty on, men eat more protein because their bodies need it to build, repair, and synthesize muscle.

Men biologically need more protein; women biologically need more sugar, fat, and chocolate. Maybe there is some truth to the nursery rhyme "Jack Sprat could eat no fat, his wife could eat no lean."

EVE'S BLESSING

All of our changes throughout life are natural, biological, and scientifically explainable. Our varying moods make us unique, sensitive, and mysterious. In the past, women were viewed as having supernatural powers. Today we are viewed as moody, unpredictable, and weak. Society doesn't understand us, most men don't understand us, even Freud had his own misunderstanding. He felt that a woman's menstrual cycle is the result of her envy and desire for the male sex organ, and her anger and frustration is let out through blood and pain. Sorry, Freud—you're not even close.

After learning about the biology of female food cravings, most of my clients are elated. "Food cravings are not a sign of weakness; they are a sign of biological advancement. They really are Eve's Blessing."

A few of my clients, however, initially feel biologically

•

doomed instead of biologically blessed. "How am I ever going to control these uncontrollable female food cravings and lose weight? I will be tempted to restrict and deprive myself even more."

But restriction isn't the answer to female food cravings and weight loss; it's the cause of uncontrollable cravings and weight gain.

•

Two

SOCIETY'S EATING RULES

LEAD TO FEMALE BLUES

ARLY IN MY CAREER, I used to recommend the traditional approach to controlling food cravings and weight: abstinence and restriction. I would ask my clients for a written commitment to abstain from chocolate (or other craved food) for a month. After some protest, they would acquiesce and vow to have the willpower to abstain, but I would eventually learn that their professed willpower was short-lived. At that time, my office was located across the street from a gourmet chocolate store, and inevitably, many of my clients would confess that once they left my office, after first making sure that I wasn't watching, they would dash across the street, buy a pound of their favorite variety, and eat the entire pound in the car on the way home.

That's what abstinence does. If the craving is biological, we need it, but if we know we can't have it, we want and need it even more.

I parted from that unsuccessful approach over ten years

•

ago, but unfortunately the restrained approach to eating is still widely practiced in our society. We have been led to believe that in order to control our food cravings, achieve a healthy diet, and attain the perfect, pencil-thin body (biologically impossible for 95 percent of all women), we must commit to the following socially accepted eating rules:

1. Eliminate the "forbidden" high-fat and high-sugar foods
2. Abstain from fulfilling food cravings
3. Follow a reduced-calorie diet
4. Avoid snacking and eat no more than 3 meals a day

A woman's body is not designed to follow restrained eating rules like these. Therefore, no matter how motivated we are, our commitment doesn't last long, and we are doomed to fail.

These eating rules have not only been unsuccessful but, more important, have jeopardized the emotional and physical benefits women can receive from food. They have caused an unnatural disruption in the balance of our bodies and minds and are responsible, at least in part, for our overwhelming fatigue, our frequent mood swings, our debilitating premenstrual and menopausal symptoms, our uncontrollable food cravings, and our struggles with weight loss that so many of us know all too well.

I will help you to break the old pattern of eating behaviors by first dispelling each of these socially accepted rules, and then, at the end of this chapter, I will update the definition of healthy eating for women. This new definition will take into consideration our efficient survival mechanism, hormonal fluctuations, blood sugar changes, brain chemical changes, and of course, our vital biological female food cravings.

•

THE MISLABELED "FORBIDDEN" FOODS

What foods do you consider strictly forbidden?

(Coincidentally, the response to this question is identical to the foods women naturally crave—chocolate, sugar, fat, and starch.)

Suzi (who was a devout Catholic) answered this question by listing the "sin" foods in her version of the 10 Food Commandments:

1. Thou shalt not eat chocolate (absolved on Valentine's Day).
2. Thou shalt not eat refined sugar (absolved with artificial sweeteners).
3. Thou shalt not eat cake (absolved on your birthday).
4. Thou shalt not eat cookies (absolved if associated with a church or school bake sale).
5. Thou shalt not eat ice cream (absolved if you are pregnant).
6. Thou shalt not eat fast food (absolved if you are under the age of 10).
7. Thou shalt not eat candy (absolved if you are over the age of 70).
8. Thou shalt not eat butter or margarine (absolved if it is labeled "diet" or "nonfat").
9. Thou shalt not eat red meat (absolved if you are of the male persuasion).
10. Thou shalt not eat snack foods (absolved if they are baked, not fried).

However we list or categorize the forbidden foods, somehow we feel as if we've committed a food "sin" when we eat them. If we eat a bad food, then we must be a bad person and deserve punishment. The usual self-inflicted punishment is either a long sentencing of restriction or a quick torture with

•

an all-out binge. Neither of these responses uses food to our biological advantage.

I know you'll be happy to hear that you don't deserve any punishment at all for fulfilling your "forbidden" food cravings. In fact, you deserve a reward. **Every food is a "good" food as long as you are responding to your body's needs with a small amount.**

"How can chocolate possibly be good for me?" asked my skeptical client Jill. "It's loaded with sugar, caffeine, fat, cholesterol, and calories. It causes tooth decay, acne, migraine headaches, and weight gain—anything that tastes that good has to be bad for you!"

For women, foods that "taste good" make us "feel good"—and therefore *are* good for us. Allow me to dispel the anti-chocolate propaganda.

1. Chocolate is *not* high in caffeine. It has only 6 mg per ounce, compared to 180 mg per 5-ounce cup of coffee.
2. Chocolate is *not* high in cholesterol. It comes from the cocoa bean, and plants do not contain any cholesterol (only animals do). Because of the added milk solids, milk chocolate does have some cholesterol, but only 7 mg per ounce, compared to 70 mg per three ounce serving of red meat.
3. The cocoa butter in chocolate does *not* raise your blood cholesterol as other saturated fats do. The cocoa butter is high in a special type of fat, stearic acid, that has actually been found to lower blood cholesterol levels in some studies.
4. Chocolate is *not* as high in calories as you may think. A Hershey's Kiss has only 25 calories—and all you need is one kiss to fulfill a biological food craving.
5. Chocolate does *not* promote tooth decay as much as other high-sugar foods do. An antibacterial agent has been re-

•

cently found in chocolate that inhibits plaque formation. Still, it is important to brush your teeth after eating chocolate.

6. Chocolate does *not* cause acne. No scientific research exists to link chocolate to skin breakouts, except for one study that had adolescents smear it on their faces instead of eat it.

7. Chocolate is *not* the primary cause of headaches; alcohol is. Some people lack an enzyme to digest the amines found in chocolate, but these amines are also found in certain fruits, milk products, meats, and alcohols.

Hooray for chocolate!!

On to the next forbidden female food—sugar. Why is sugar considered bad? Judith answered this question with a dissertation about the sins of sugar. "Sugar is white death. It causes diabetes, hyperactivity, depression, hypoglycemia, stress, yeast infections, nutrient depletion, and tooth decay."

WOW! Then why do we have taste buds for sugar? Why do children love sugar? Ninety-nine percent of all the ills attributed to sugar are unfounded. Medical research has disproved the connection between sugar and diabetes (sugar is not the cause of diabetes, but reducing sugar intake is a part of the treatment), depression, hypoglycemia, and nutrient depletion. Even the sugar/hyperactivity connection has been disproven, and recently, sugar has been found to calm hyperactive kids and quiet a crying baby. The only problem with sugar that holds true is that it causes cavities—so brush your teeth after eating it.

Despite the research that defends eating sugar in moderation, the myths still prevail. Sugar has always been around. Years ago, the riper the berries, the better. Today, the sweeter the dessert, the better. Of course, too much sugar,

•

just as too much of anything, will cause weight gain and other problems. But if you are craving it and you satisfy that craving with a small amount, it will calm you, relax you, and stabilize you.

Sugar has been labeled bad for the past thirty years or so, but now fat is rapidly taking its place. The message is loud and clear: Fat causes heart disease and cancer and is hazardous to your health. Trim, cut, substitute, reduce—eliminate it from your diet. So we try, but we can't seem to follow a very low-fat diet successfully for long. We don't lose much weight; we don't feel so great; and we crave fat despite our efforts. Why?

- Women need some fat for our survival mechanism.
- Women need some fat to prepare for pregnancy and breast-feeding.
- Women need some fat to keep fat cells happy.
- Women need some fat to keep brain cells happy.

The current race to cut fat to 10 percent or less of our daily calories may work for men, but it doesn't work for most women. From my experience, women last about a month at best on a 10 percent fat diet and then they go to a 50 percent fat diet in rebellion. A restricted-fat diet creates its own little famine. We are not taking in what we need for survival, so our bodies rebel by reducing brain chemicals, reducing metabolism, and stimulating fat cravings.

Too much fat isn't healthy for anyone—but we need a little more fat in our diets than men do to keep our fat cells happy with stored fat and to keep our brain cells happy with endorphins.

We've discussed chocolate, sugar, and fat—but I think it may be necessary to dispel the belief that starch is also a "for-

•

bidden" food. Although many women have come to realize that starches are a healthy choice, many others still believe that breads, cereals, pasta, and rice are fattening and cause weight gain.

Since the first weight-loss diet was created, starches have been viewed as an enemy instead of an ally. Fifty-odd years ago, someone (I won't mention any names) decided breads, pasta, rice, and potatoes were fattening. Even though starches have since been proven to promote weight loss, "fattening" reputations are hard to change and myths still periodically surface.

Don't believe any of the myths you hear about bread or any other high-starch food. Starches do not cause weight gain unless you overeat them (overeating *any* food will cause weight gain). Pasta does not go straight to the hips. Bread does not stick to the stomach. But—all of these high-starch foods will fuel your body, stabilize your blood sugar, and enhance your moods. As you will discover in Chapter 5, starch is not an enemy, but rather a strong ally because it is your brain's longtime companion.

So, chocolate, sugar, fat, and starch aren't forbidden foods at all—*they are pleasure foods for a woman's body*. I'll never suggest that you eat a pound of chocolate or a quart of ice cream. I will, however, strongly suggest that you listen to your body and respond to its needs. If what your body biologically needs is chocolate or potato chips, a small amount will do the trick. They won't be stored in your fat cells, they won't clog your arteries, they won't increase your risk of cancer. Instead, your body will use these foods for all its biological needs.

You do not need to abstain from your female pleasure foods. When you try, it usually backfires.

•

ABSTINENCE MAKES THE CRAVING GROW STRONGER

You may have tried a number of abstinence techniques, but have any of them worked? No, and most likely they have had the opposite effect. Instead of alleviating the craving, abstinence escalates the craving.

Here's what happens when you try to abstain from a biological food craving:

Your brain first gives you a subtle message: "Please give me some chocolate."

You say, "No way, I'm on a diet trying to lose weight. Here, have an apple instead."

Your brain says, "Sorry, I don't need an apple. I need chocolate and I need it right this very minute."

You say, "I can do it. I can have the willpower," but as you continue with the self-talk, you are feeling more preoccupied, anxious, and depressed.

Now your brain is banging on the bongos to get you to pay attention. "You blew it. Now that you've denied me, you need five pieces of chocolate to make up for the wait. An hour ago, I would have been perfectly satisfied with one piece."

Abstinence causes overindulgence. Now you've overeaten, you feel guilty, you have a stomachache, and your blood sugar is out of whack. You fear weight gain, so you vow to fast for the next twenty-four hours. A bad decision: You are now propelled into a cycle that is difficult to break out of.

•

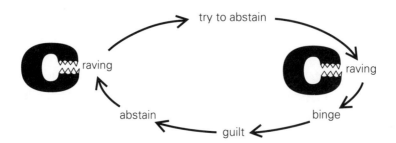

Abstinence does not make your heart, mood, or brain grow fonder. It only makes your cravings grow stronger.

DIETING AND BRAIN TURBULENCE

Diets don't work for at least a hundred reasons. Here's reason number 101:

Dieting causes brain turbulence: It decreases your brain chemicals and brain sugar supply, increases your food cravings, and depresses your mood. Dieting is really one long period of abstinence.

You may ask, "Is that why my family runs for cover when they hear that I started a new diet? Is that why my PMS symptoms are worse when I'm dieting? Is that why I inevitably end my diet with a fat/sugar binge?"

The answer to all of the above: Yes.

Yet we have been led to believe that in order to lose weight, we must diet. If one diet doesn't work, try another one. If that one didn't work, try the liquid meals. If they don't work, try fasting for the rest of your life.

In any given month, 35 percent of all women are on a diet. If you are one of the 35 percent this month, please give it up now. The diet has a 98 percent chance of failing anyway, and a 100 percent chance of causing havoc in your body.

When you diet, your brain registers "FAMINE" and to ensure your survival, the biochemical changes begin. You

•

may know that death is not pending, but your body doesn't. Your brain has a built-in monitoring device that detects insufficient calories. When you're taking in too few calories, your brain gets nervous and decides you need to take in more. Your metabolism and serotonin levels begin to drop, and your thoughts and cravings turn to something sweet and gooey. You try not to respond so you lock the refrigerator, call up your diet counselor, or pray to a higher being.

Of course, nothing works. Our bodies want to protect the stored fat and our brains lend a helping hand by stimulating sugar and fat cravings. Some studies have shown that sugar and fat intake can as much as double after the diet is over.

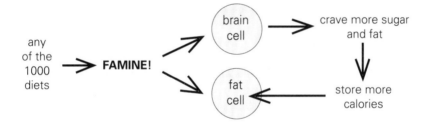

Diet today, deal with brain turbulence and weight gain tomorrow. Dieting throws your routine completely out of synch. **You didn't fail the diet. The diet failed you.** You have no control over the way your brain and body respond to a diet. The only thing you can control is the decision never to diet again for the rest of your life.

And you thought the bad news about dieting was over.

THE BALANCED MEAL APPROACH DOES NOT BALANCE A WOMAN'S MOOD

Do not snack! Eat three balanced meals a day! Breakfast is the most important meal of the day! The dinner meal must include protein, starch, vegetable, milk, bread, and salad!

•

These are all familiar phrases. We have been hearing them since childhood, and children are still taught this balanced-meal approach to healthy eating. Nonetheless, this approach to healthy eating is the direct opposite of what the female body needs. Based on our hormones, blood-sugar needs, and brain chemical balance—**we need to snack, eat small, frequent meals throughout the day, de-emphasize dinner, and emphasize lunch.**

As you will soon discover, lunch wins the "most important meal of the day award" for helping a woman to function optimally. First of all, women don't realize this, and second of all our eating rules have disregarded lunch to focus instead on breakfast and dinner. Lunch has gotten lost in the hustle and bustle of day-to-day living.

What we choose to eat (or not eat) at lunchtime can have a profound effect on energy, productivity, and moods for the rest of the day. But what do *you* eat for lunch? Here are some responses to this question:

- "Nothing, that's the meal I skip every day."
- "One of those weight-loss drinks."
- "A salad with nonfat dressing."
- "Nonfat frozen yogurt."
- "Whatever I have time for, usually fast food.

That's one of the problems: We don't have time to focus on lunch. We don't realize how very important lunch is to our minds and moods, and we barely allow thirty minutes for lunch. We run around doing errands for everyone else, then we eat quickly or don't even take a lunch break at all. The result is an afternoon of fatigue, lack of concentration, and difficulty handling stress.

We do, however, have plenty of time for a leisurely, large

•

dinner. Actually, a large, late dinner throws off our biochemistry and biological rhythms. If we eat a large dinner, we are not hungry in the morning, we eat a small lunch, and then because we have to make up for the lack of food during the day, our dinner meal becomes even larger.

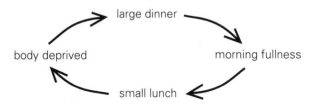

Many other cultures listen to their bodies, eat their main meal midday, and snack frequently. The French eat their largest meal in the afternoon and are always researched for their lower weights and lower risk of heart disease despite their high-fat and high-cholesterol diets. England and Spain have built in snack times with the afternoon tea and tapas. Most of the European countries consume even more chocolate than we do, but they weigh less. Chocolate isn't causing any problems because they are eating in accordance with their body's needs.

The traditional balanced-meal approach does not balance your moods. It does create an imbalance in your energy, moods, and brain chemistry.

FOR WOMEN ONLY: THE NEW, IMPROVED HEALTHY EATING RULES

Now that we have dispelled all the myths, I hope you are convinced that the restrained eating rules have not only restrained your innate ability to use food to your biological advantage, but they are also the cause of overindulgence.

•

Because women cannot follow restrictive eating habits for long and then feel guilty when they do give in to their biological food cravings, research is showing that more and more women are resorting to secretive eating to fulfill their needs.

According to the most recent national nutrition surveys, what we are eating and what we say we are eating doesn't match up. We are reporting that we are eating less chocolate, desserts, and chips—but the food consumption data shows that our intakes of these foods have increased by 17 percent over the last ten years!

We have successfully reduced our red meat consumption, but that should come as no surprise since a woman's body needs less protein anyway. However, a woman's body does need chocolate, fat, and sugar—and that's why when we try to follow a restrictive diet, it often backfires, and we end up eating more when no one is around. Restriction is the cause of overconsumption!

You do not have to go into hiding any longer to fulfill your female food needs. With your newfound knowledge, you can begin honoring your body and respecting your food cravings for the important messages they provide. You *can* fulfill your female food needs and achieve a healthier diet at the same time!

In fact, if the socially accepted restrained eating rules never existed and we were free to choose foods based on our instinctive needs, we would automatically eat a healthier diet that is best suited for our female bodies:

- We would choose 60% to 70% of our daily intake from carbohydrates, mostly starches and some sugar (currently it's only 46%).
- We would choose 20% to 30% of our daily intake from fats (currently it's 37%).

•

- We would choose only 10% to 15% of our daily intake from protein (currently it's 17%).
- We would eat 5 small meals and snacks a day with a special focus on lunch (currently it's 2½ meals).

We would be eating double the meals (but smaller), more carbohydrates and vegetables, and less fat and protein!

Let's update the eating rules to take a woman's body, mind, and natural eating instincts into consideration:

1. No food is forbidden. Any food is an acceptable choice when we respond to our body's needs with a moderate amount.
2. Eat chocolate in moderation.
3. Eat sugar in moderation.
4. Eat fat in moderation.
5. Focus on starch.
6. Eat 5 times a day—snacking is encouraged.
7. Emphasize lunch and de-emphasize dinner.

This is every woman's optimal eating routine that will put your mind, moods, and body back *on* track. From now on, we'll call this eating routine the **ON** Plan: **O**ptimal **N**utrition for Mind and Body. The **ON** Plan will turn *on* your instinctive food needs, turn *on* your positive moods, and turn *on* your healthy body. For so long, we have been working against our natural female appetite. Let's begin working with our female food needs and taking responsibility for our own well-being. The **ON** Plan is just the tool you need to get started.

•

Three

THE **ON** PLAN:

OPTIMAL NUTRITION

FOR MIND AND BODY

"FOR THE PAST FIFTEEN YEARS I have been trying to follow the restrained approach to healthy eating without much success, but now I've learned that my lack of success had to do not with me, but with the approach. I've not only been ignoring my female food needs, but I have also caused my mind and body to work separately. Can I undo the damage?"

Absolutely! That's what the **ON** Plan is all about—reconnecting your mind and body and putting you back in touch with your instinctive food needs.

It doesn't matter how long you've been dieting, denying, and skipping meals. What's most important is your new understanding of the female body and how those past restrained eating rules have only inhibited your inborn biological food advantage. They have minimized your mood, increased your weight, and belittled your body.

•

The Past Restrained Eating Rules

You can reverse direction and transform restraint into re-vitalization with the **ON** Plan. You can maximize your moods, boost your energy, and benefit your body by turning your female food cravings and instinctive food needs back on.

The ON Plan

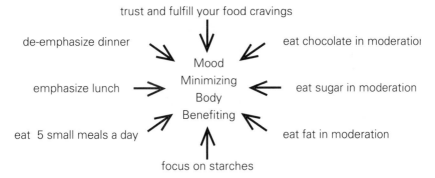

The **ON** Plan is the optimal nutrition solution for every woman in every sense of the word. Optimal for turning *on* your:

> positive moods
> creative mind
> productive energy
> healthy body

•

comfortable weight
instinctive food needs
female food cravings
enjoyment and pleasure from food

Optimal nutrition for women is eating what we *crave* (whatever it is, including sugar, fat, chocolate, and starch), and eating *five* times a day. This plan may at first seem to go against everything you've ever heard or read. Often women ask me, "What kind of nutritionist are you?"

I am a "woman's nutritionist" who is dedicated to helping women take care of themselves by looking and feeling as good as they possibly can. If you are feeling great with what you are eating, then you don't need the **ON** Plan. But . . .

- if you are one of the 92% of all women who report chronic fatigue, mood swings, and depression
- if you are one of the 90% of all women who experience premenstrual or menopausal tension
- If you are one of the 85% of all women who are unhappy with their weight
- If you are one of the 78% of all women who have an unhealthy relationship with food

> . . . then you *need* the **ON** Plan.

So, what exactly is the **ON** Plan?

Before describing the five steps to optimal nutrition, I need to share with you an important philosophy that is integral to the success of the plan—**PLEASURE. The first goal is to take the guilt out of eating and put the pleasure back in.**

•

THE PRINCIPLES OF PLEASURE EATING

"What in the world is 'pleasure eating'? I don't think I've had a completely pleasurable eating experience since I was nine years old. Even if I enjoy the taste of the food, the over-whelming guilt I feel afterward takes away any pleasure."

Far too often, guilt is the feeling attached to eating. It clouds our common sense and consumes our thoughts. Sue still feels guilty about the chocolate cake that she ate two years ago. Some women feel guilty before, during, and after eating, which makes the eating experience completely void of pleasure.

Do you know which are your guilt-producing foods? For Sue and many other women, it's chocolate. "I think 'guilt' is listed as one of the ingredients right after cocoa butter. Anything with fat, sugar, or salt produces guilt. Anything canned, frozen, or processed produces guilt because we are supposed to eat fresh foods. Even bananas make me feel guilty because they are the highest calorie fruit."

Bananas? Many women avoid bananas because they believe the calorie content is high. Bananas have only twenty more calories than an apple, but they also have 300 percent more potassium. Give bananas a break. If we try hard enough, we can find a reason to feel guilty about eating any food. Some of my clients have gone to the extreme of labeling "food" a four-letter word.

Think of the last time you had a pleasurable eating experience. What did you eat? Why did you eat it? What did it feel like? How long ago was it?

Here are Ann's responses to these questions. "It was the Thanksgiving before last (last Thanksgiving was at my house so the work interfered with the pleasure). I ate my aunt's incredible stuffing and my mom's delectable pumpkin pie.

•

That's what I wanted, I enjoyed every exploding mouthful, and I had a great time with the family afterward. I didn't feel guilty because Thanksgiving is the only day of the year that I allow myself to eat whatever I want."

Eating pleasure for Ann happened only once a year; on the other 364 days, she felt restricted, deprived, or guilty.

Like Ann, I too used to restrict and deprive. But now pleasure is a goal of just about every eating experience. I think about what will be most satisfying to me and strive for satisfaction. My husband knows when it's a "turbo-satisfying" meal because he sees me do what he calls the "happy dance" where I shake my shoulders back and forth in delight. If I were to choose one meal that wins the pleasure award, it would have to be a pizza-and-potato-chip party when my husband is out of town. It's not that I'm happiest when my husband is out of town (despite what my friends may tell you), but it is nice every now and then to have personal, uninterrupted space with my pizza and potato chips.

Think of someone you know who derives consistent pleasure and satisfaction from food, and talk to her about it. Does she feel guilty about eating being a pleasurable experience? What does she eat? How does she eat it? Is she overweight?

Stephanie thought of her friend Lori: "When I go to a restaurant with her, she analyzes the menu for at least fifteen minutes trying to decide what will be most satisfying to her. Sometimes it's the pasta and other times it's the filet mignon. She's fit, she's at a moderate weight, she's guilt-free, and she's a blast to be with."

You too can have the same experiences. **You can replace guilt with pleasure!**

Throughout the **ON** Plan, we will use the principles of pleasure eating to guide us:

•

The Principles of Pleasure Eating

1. Define your cravings as healthy, natural messages to balance mind and body.
2. Think fulfillment, not control.
3. Eat exactly what you want, crave, and desire.
4. Release the guilt, embrace the pleasure.
5. Experience satisfaction with each and every meal.

Eating provides pleasure in all of our lives, but the pleasure women can potentially receive from food is far greater than ever imagined. With the **ON** Plan, you will take that pleasure potential to its limits. You will be neither restricting what you eat nor binging, both of which take away the pleasure attached to eating and negatively affect your female body and brain. Instead, you will find the right balance wherein food provides the immediate mental benefits as well as the long-term physical benefits. There is an optimal middle ground for our all-or-nothing mentality—and I'll help you find that pleasurable middle ground with the five progressive steps of the **ON** Plan.

THE FIVE STEPS TO OPTIMAL NUTRITION FOR MIND AND BODY

For the next five weeks, we will use these five principles of pleasure eating in combination with the five progressive steps of the **ON** Plan. By doing so, you will gain the necessary trust, awareness, and skills to help you feel as good as you possibly can while nourishing your female body. The positive changes you'll experience in your mind and body during these five weeks will make you want to continue with the plan for the rest of your life. Here's a preview of the next five weeks:

•

STEP 1: TRUST YOUR FEMALE FOOD CRAVINGS The first step is always the most difficult, but also the most important because it prepares you to receive maximum benefit from the rest of the plan. You can't improve mood, energy, and vitality without trusting your food instincts. Many women fear weight gain, loss of control, binge eating, and increased risk of disease. I will help you to realistically overcome all of your food craving fears and to accurately differentiate between a biological food craving and an emotional food craving.

STEP 2: DISCOVER YOUR FEMALE PLEASURE FOODS Some of you may already have a good sense of what foods make you energetic, happy, and productive. But many of you will have to spend some time experimenting with foods to become aware of how they influence your mind and body. Through a full and uncomplicated understanding of how certain foods affect your brain and body, you'll be able to identify your pleasure food list.

STEP 3: LEARN HOW TO EAT FOR MAXIMUM SATISFACTION Next, we'll take your personal pleasure foods and teach you how to eat them to derive the most satisfaction and benefit: in your taste buds, stomach, body, and brain. You'll also learn to identify factors that can interfere with your level of satisfaction—searching for substitutes, eating too much protein, and eating too much of your pleasure foods.

STEP 4: DISTRIBUTE YOUR FOOD TO MAXIMIZE MOOD Now that you know *what* to eat, *how* to eat, and *how much* to eat, the next step is *when* to eat. Timing is of greatest importance to receive the maximum benefit in your mood, energy,

•

and productivity. Certain times of the day are most important for fulfilling your food cravings, and certain meals of the day are essential to emphasize.

STEP 5: FOLLOW YOUR OPTIMAL EATING ROUTINE
This is your final step to use food to your full biological advantage. It's your optimal eating routine that will balance your brain and body daily, monthly, and yearly—and when your brain is under considerable strain because of stress, sleep deprivation, and the shorter days of the winter months.

The **ON** Plan is for all women of all ages, from puberty through postmenopause. It will help you to get back in touch with your instinctive food needs and your optimal eating routine. For so long, we have relied on external signals for eating: society's rules, the clock, the diet plan. We have been programmed with dietary instructions that are out of synch with our body's needs. Let your body guide you to **O**ptimal **N**utrition with these five progressive steps:

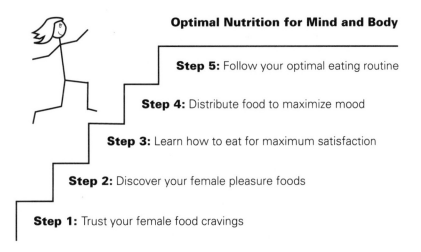

Optimal Nutrition for Mind and Body

Step 5: Follow your optimal eating routine

Step 4: Distribute food to maximize mood

Step 3: Learn how to eat for maximum satisfaction

Step 2: Discover your female pleasure foods

Step 1: Trust your female food cravings

•

It's all about finding and following an eating routine that is optimal for *you*.

Why do you need to find it? Why can't I just tell you the best routine? Because it's different for each of us. What is an optimal routine for me may not be optimal for you. It all depends on where you are today and how much your routine has been disrupted by restrained eating and your personal lifestyle.

If you've been skipping breakfast for the past ten years, your body and mind has been off kilter for ten years. If you've been dieting most of your life, your body doesn't even know there is such a thing as an optimal eating routine. If you've been denying your food cravings, your body is attempting to lead you toward a routine, but you are trying to fight it.

Whatever your current and past eating habits, each of you will discover an eating routine that is best for you with the **ON** Plan.

As an example, this is the optimal eating routine that Lauren personally discovered. She initially came to see me with the goal of weight loss. But as with most clients, many other goals were uncovered along the way. She was also in counseling for depression, was chronically fatigued, and was obsessed with food. With her past dieting practices, binging behavior, and panic about food and calories, she was as far away from the positive food-mood connection as any of my clients. At one level she was an intuitive woman with amazing insight and perception, but when it came to food and her body, she was disassociated and out of touch. Then she came down with the flu and was sick for four days. During that time, her eating behavior was amazingly different. She only wanted bagels, oatmeal, and noodles during the day, something sweet at 4:00 P.M., and she could care less about dinner. If her body wanted anything at night, it was protein. As she

•

was telling (or confessing) this to me, she noticed my look of excitement. I told her that her routine was perfect—this was how I wanted her to eat all the time.

Her response was, "But I ate some sugar every day, and bagels, oatmeal, and noodles are fattening." Even though she felt more stable and in control of her eating, she actually felt guilty because she was so concerned about her weight.

WILL THIS PLAN HELP ME LOSE WEIGHT?

This is the big question—one that at least 99 percent of all women ask me. The answer is . . . yes!

Responding to your body's instinctive food needs means listening to your body's hunger signals (I'll help you to identify hunger signals in the first step), and then eating what your body wants when it's hungry. And of course, not overeating. The **ON** Plan *will* result in permanent weight loss.

If you want to lose weight, you have to eat and respond to your body's food signals. If you want to gain weight, continue dieting and denying your food needs. As a matter of fact, one of the most successful ways to gain weight is to practice yo-yo dieting. Each time you go off a diet and back to your old eating habits, you gain the weight back—plus some. The average woman has lost 100 pounds by dieting, only to regain 125 pounds.

If you read my first book, *Outsmarting the Female Fat Cell*, you now realize that the strategies of the **OFF** Plan to **O**utsmart **F**emale **F**at are complementary to the steps of the **ON** Plan for **O**ptimal **N**utrition. A woman's body must be treated differently from a man's in regard to weight loss and enhanced emotional well-being. By working with our unique physiology, you can accomplish all of your goals.

•

The **ON** Plan for Optimal Nutrition	The **OFF** Plan for Weight Loss
Don't deprive yourself.	Stop dieting and start eating.
Listen to your body and fulfill your food cravings.	Eat what you want when you are hungry, just don't overeat.
Eat 5 small meals a day.	Shrink and multiply your meals.
Focus on lunch.	Become a daytime eater.
Eat a moderate amount of fat.	Balance your fat intake.
Exercise for endorphins.	Exercise for fat loss.

Exercise? I haven't discussed exercise yet in this book, but you may as well prepare yourself now because there is an entire chapter on it. Exercise is so vital to a woman's well-being that we could consider it the 6th step of the **ON** Plan. That's all I'll say for now.

I find it most intriguing that by following the **ON** Plan, women report less frequent and less intense food cravings. The reason: Your brain is constantly content, so it doesn't have to send you messages as often. And when it does send you messages, they are pleasant, subtle, and manageable. You didn't need the package of cookies; 2 cookies satisfied you. You didn't devour the quart of ice cream, a scoop did the trick.

The ON Plan encourages self-indulgence without overindulgence, and, therefore, promotes weight loss.

You can stabilize moods while stabilizing weight. You can gain energy while losing weight. You can **turn off** your fat cells while **turning on** your productive brain cells. You can look good while feeling great.

Healthy eating—for your mind, your body, and your weight—can *all* be achieved with the **ON** Plan.

•

ARE YOU READY FOR THE <u>ON</u> PLAN?

"Am I ready? I've been waiting for someone to finally validate my food awarenesses and address my special female needs. I was ready for the **ON** Plan ten years ago. I'm ready to start this very minute."

Most women are so empowered by the understanding of female food cravings and their instinctive food needs that they are almost too ready. I want you to take things slowly over the next five weeks. There is so much to learn and so much to experience along the way.

And, before you begin, I want to prepare you for the **ON** Plan. Before you can effectively turn on your female food cravings, positive moods, productive energy, and renewed vitality, you must understand how much society and your current eating behaviors have turned them off. The following questionnaires on each of the five **ON** steps will help you gain a greater awareness of yourself, your eating habits, and how important each of these steps will be for you.

•

STEP 1: TRUST YOUR FEMALE FOOD CRAVINGS

Rate the following statements as follows:
0—never
1—seldom
2—frequently
3—always

1. I try to deny my food cravings. _____

2. I diet to lose weight. _____

3. Once I start eating, I have a difficult time
stopping. _____

4. If I fulfill my food cravings, I fear weight
gain. _____

5. If I fulfill my food cravings, I fear that I'll
have an unhealthy diet. _____

6. I label foods as "good" or "bad." _____

7. I feel guilty after eating the foods I crave. _____

8. I eat my pleasure foods when no one is
around. _____

9. I feel that I lack willpower and discipline. _____

10. I eat for emotional reasons. _____

TOTAL _____

•

STEP 2: DISCOVER YOUR FEMALE PLEASURE FOODS

Rate each of the statements as follows:
0—never
1—seldom
2—frequently
3—always

1. I restrict chocolate in my diet. _____

2. I restrict sugar in my diet. _____

3. I restrict starch in my diet. _____

4. I restrict fat in my diet. _____

5. I restrict salt in my diet. _____

6. I feel that carbohydrates are fattening. _____

7. I try to find "healthier" substitutes for my food cravings. _____

8. I use sugar for a quick pick-me-up. _____

9. I try to follow a very low-sugar diet. _____

10. I try to follow a very low-fat diet. _____

TOTAL _____

•

STEP 3: LEARN HOW TO EAT FOR MAXIMUM SATISFACTION

Rate each of the statements as follows:
0—never
1—seldom
2—frequently
3—always

1. I eat quickly. _____

2. I barely chew my food. _____

3. I eat standing up. _____

4. I eat unconsciously. _____

5. I overeat the foods I crave. _____

6. I clean my plate. _____

7. My meals contain a protein source, starch, salad, and vegetable. _____

8. I use artificial sweeteners. _____

9. I buy "nonfat" foods. _____

10. I don't feel satisfied with food. _____

TOTAL _____

•

STEP 4: DISTRIBUTE YOUR FOOD TO MAXIMIZE MOOD

Rate each of the statements as follows:
0—never
1—seldom
2—frequently
3—always

1. I skip breakfast.   _____

2. I skip lunch.   _____

3. My biggest meal is dinner.   _____

4. My food cravings are strongest in the
   evening.   _____

5. I eat dinner after 7:00 P.M.   _____

6. I feel that snacking is "bad."   _____

7. I eat 3 times (or fewer) a day.   _____

8. I snack before going to bed.   _____

9. I drink more than 2 cups of regular coffee a
   day.   _____

10. I don't have time for a leisurely lunch.   _____

                                        TOTAL   _____

•

STEP 5: FOLLOW YOUR OPTIMAL EATING ROUTINE

Rate each of the statements as follows:
0—never
1—seldom
2—frequently
3—always

1. I have daily mood swings. _____

2. I have overwhelming fatigue. _____

3. I experience the 3:30 P.M. slump. _____

4. I'm depressed during the winter months. _____

5. I have difficulty sleeping at night. _____

6. I experience PMS or menopausal tension. _____

7. I crave more foods during the winter months. _____

8. I crave more foods during PMS or menopause. _____

9. I eat more sugar and fat when I am stressed. _____

10. I have difficulty controlling my weight. _____

TOTAL _____

•

The higher you scored on these questionnaires, the more benefit you will receive from applying the **ON** Plan to your life. Those steps that you scored highest on will be the most important as you work through the next 5 weeks. List your scores from the previous pages and add up the total.

WHAT WERE YOUR SCORES?

SCORES

Step 1: Trust Your Female Food Cravings _____

Step 2: Discover Your Female Pleasure Foods _____

Step 3: Learn How to Eat for Maximum Satisfaction _____

Step 4: Distribute Your Food to Maximize Mood _____

Step 5: Follow Your Optimal Eating Routine _____

TOTAL SCORE _____

"I got the highest possible score—150 points! Do I get a prize or a penalty? Has anyone else ever scored that high?"

If this was your questionnaire result, no need to worry. Many women score well over 100 points. A high score doesn't make you a bad person. It's only an indication of the benefits you will receive from the **ON** Plan. The higher your score, the more you *need* the **ON** Plan, and the better you'll feel and function when you make it a part of your life.

Now you *are* ready for the **ON** Plan. You have the understanding of your female food cravings, your female brain chemistry, and your instinctive female food needs. You have the awareness of society's neglect and the negative influence of the universally accepted eating rules. And now you have the awareness of your attitudes and habits and which of the **ON** steps will be most important for you.

Turn the page and begin turning on your optimal eating routine.

•

Four

I F YOU WERE GOING ON A wilderness excursion in the backcountry (even if you never would, just pretend), would you trust a guide without experience? Would you choose a guide who was really a banker doing backpacking on the side? Of course not. You would make sure that you had an experienced, dependable, and knowledgeable person to lead you into unknown territory.

Well, you are venturing into new territory with the **ON** Plan, and your body is the dependable guide. It's the expert in directing you down the path to weight loss, optimal health, and mood enhancement. But, in order for your body to use its expertise, you must trust its food messages and listen to them.

For some of us, however, trust may be an unknown terrain and a bit frightening. This fear isn't surprising since for so long, we have been taught not to trust our internal messages and instincts and to rely instead on the external guidance of other people, diets, plans, programs, clinics, books, articles,

•

and infomercials. Well, nobody except *you* knows what's optimal for your body and mind.

If, like some of my clients, trust in yourself is something that you think you don't have, I'll show you that you *do* have it, but right now it's just buried beneath some fears and uncertainties. First, I'll help you strip away the most common food craving fears:

- "Once I start eating, I won't be able to stop."
- "I'll gain weight."
- "My diet will be unhealthy."

And then—I'll address the uncertainty of not knowing whether the craving is biologically or emotionally driven. If you are sometimes not sure and ask the question: "Is it body hunger or heart hunger?" I'll help you answer it confidently.

You can replace fear with knowledge and uncertainty with confidence. You *can* trust your food cravings!

ONCE YOU START EATING, YOU *CAN* STOP

How many times have you heard the potato chip commercial telling you that "you can't eat just one"? Eventually, you start to believe it about chips and most other foods. Once you eat one, you'll end up eating the entire bag, box, or container.

Well, you *can* eat just one and be perfectly satisfied, go on with life, and fulfill your female food needs. I'm not necessarily asking you to eat just one potato chip, but you certainly don't need the entire bag. A small handful will produce all the satisfaction you want. If you do "feel" like you can't stop eating and need to eat the entire one-pound bag, something other than your internal biological needs is driving your appetite.

•

67

My clients often label these other needs as "binge" voices that lead them to believe they can't eat just one and keep reminding them that they don't have control. Sometimes the voices are from the distant past, and sometimes they are soft whispers instead of loud yells, but until you identify them, confront them, and quiet them, they are always there to stifle your trust. Here are some of my clients' "binge" voices.

The Deprivation Wail

Deprivation cries out for indulgence.

I've discussed the ramifications of deprivation a number of times, but let's take a worst-case deprivation scenario with chocolate. If starting at midnight tonight, chocolate were deemed illegal, what would you do? I know what I would do: grab my car keys, race to the nearest store, fill my trunk with any and all varieties of chocolate, and devour as much as I could until the bell tolled 12:00 A.M.. I would respond as if it were a national emergency while my husband (because most men don't have the deprivation "binge" voice) would more likely shrug his shoulders and turn on ESPN.

If instead, chocolate were deemed the healthiest food in the world and we could eat it morning, noon, and night—that deprivation voice would fade away entirely, and we probably would never overeat chocolate again.

It's human nature; you always want what you can't have, and you never want what you can have.

The Empty Stomach Scream

Intense hunger makes your food cravings stronger, and your perceived food needs larger. If you are famished when you start eating, the empty stomach scream makes you eat a lot of food very quickly and unconsciously. Your body is trying to make up for the food you didn't give it two hours ago. When

•

you are overhungry, a small amount of food never seems to be enough. When you are moderately hungry, a small amount is usually enough.

The Food Race Roar

Rebecca knew exactly where her "binge" voice originated. "I grew up in a family of five kids, me and four hungry brothers. When my mother got home from the grocery store, it was a race to the cupboards to get to the goodies and eat as much of them as you could before someone else did. It was the "you snooze, you lose" way of life. Now I'm twenty-nine years old and live alone, but I still vacuum out the cupboards for fear that the food will somehow supernaturally disappear before I have a chance to eat it."

By acknowledging her childhood eating experience, Rebecca came to the conclusion that she didn't need to listen to her food-race voice any longer.

If it's not a food race with others, then maybe it's one with yourself. If there is a carrot cake sitting on the kitchen counter, that "binge" voice may urge you to "eat it all now as fast as you can while you have the chance—because you may not be presented with this opportunity again."

The Starving Children Broadcast

Sharon's "binge" voice came from food waste guilt. "I can't control the amount I eat because my mother was always talking at the dinner table about world hunger and starving children. Today I feel so guilty throwing away food that I eat every morsel." When Sharon realized that she could prepare less, eat less, and waste less, her mind was put at ease. She also came to the realization that whether the food was going into her stomach (and eventually into her fat cells) or into the garbage can, it wasn't going to the starving children in the world.

•

As she put it, "It either goes to my waist or in the waste—the choice is mine."

The Emotional Outcry

Sometimes the origin of the "binge" voice is an emotion striving to be felt. The heart is crying out to be nurtured, but we may literally try to stuff the sadness or anger back down with food. When food is used to distract you from feeling and the craving is emotional, a small amount is never enough. I will discuss emotional eating in more depth at the end of this chapter.

The Self-Fulfilling Prophecy

If you label yourself a "sugar addict" or a "chocoholic," you may start to exhibit addictive behaviors. First you try to eliminate sugar from your diet, then you crave sugar more often, and finally you can't seem to control your sugar binges. If food addictions do exist, they affect less than one percent of the population. Instead of labeling yourself an addict and encouraging the "self-fulfilling" voice, change your image by starting to call yourself "an educated sugar consumer" or a "chocolate connoisseur."

The Binge Food Bellow

The last "binge" voice is one that comes from the binge food itself, one (or several) more difficult for you to eat in small amounts because it seems to beckon you. Cheryl claimed that tortilla chips had vocal cords and would call to her every night at 10:00 P.M. "Cheryl, this is your favorite one-pound bag of tortilla chips calling. I'm in the cupboard right behind the nonfat rice cakes—come and get me. Oh, and don't forget the salsa."

Maybe a particular food doesn't personally talk to you,

•

but, for some reason, it may appear to zap your control and trigger a binge. For Amanda, it was potato chips. "I never keep them in the cupboard, I forbade my husband to eat them around me, and I have absolutely no control over the amount that I eat." Amanda's idea of keeping the potato chips out of sight, and, therefore, out of mind is one way to deal with it. Then again, if you crave it and are forced to deprive yourself because it's not around, the plan could backfire.

Maybe you "can't eat just one" because you've never been told that's all you need. Biochemically, your brain and body will be happy with one piece of chocolate. Eating ten pieces will not produce ten times the benefit. Eating one piece will produce the maximum benefit. Just realizing this may be enough to overcome the out-of-control-eating fear.

Identifying these and other binge voices will reduce their influence on the amount you eat. When these voices are found out, they often retreat on their own. If they persist, try the "Morning Experiment"—take a small amount of your "binge" food and eat it for breakfast. Overeating seldom occurs in the morning, so the goal is to eat the food without losing control.

I suggested that Cheryl (the talking-tortilla-chip client) try the "Morning Experiment" and eat a handful of chips with her oatmeal cereal. I know that it sounds a bit strange, but this technique helped her to realize that she could eat her craved foods without losing control with a binge.

It worked so well that three days later, she called me with a progress report. "I'm truly amazed. I've never eaten less than half a bag of tortilla chips at one sitting, but in the morning it was surprisingly easy to stop after one handful. Now I know that I can do it any time of the day and still be completely satisfied. My only fear is that I'll eat chips every day and gain weight."

•

YOU WILL *NOT* GAIN WEIGHT

Weight gain is, by far, the number-one food-craving fear for women. This should come as no surprise since in general weight gain is a top fear for all women, whether it's in relation to food cravings or not. In fact, the three top fears for women are weight gain, public speaking, and death. So, I suppose the worst possible scenario would be to give a lecture about death and dying while 100 pounds overweight. Let's deal with one fear at a time.

Deprivation, restriction, and dieting are what cause weight gain. Trusting and satisfying your cravings will not lead to weight gain and, if you have weight to lose, the **ON** Plan will help you to shed those unwanted pounds.

"But what about my passion for chocolate, bread, and sugar? I know that chocolate goes straight to my hips, bread to my stomach, and sugar to my thighs. Fulfilling my food cravings means an immediate 10-pound weight gain below the waist." As I explained to Jackie, denying food cravings is what leads to weight gain because of the inevitable sequence of these behaviors.

crave a food → deny → **C**ravings intensify → overeat → weight gain

As you start to gain weight because of denial and then overeating, the cravings become the scapegoat. You blame the sugar and chocolate cravings for your expanding waistline and protruding stomach. Then your mounting frustration and fear of further weight gain cause you to deny and restrict even more, eventually eat more, and ultimately gain more.

•

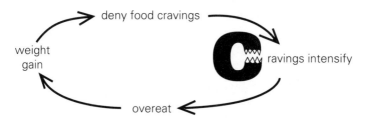

Another cycle. A cycle has a life of its own. Once it starts, it propels like a whirlpool—unless you do something to break out of it. If you stop denying your food cravings, you stop the cycle.

Food cravings don't cause weight gain; denying the cravings causes weight gain.

Wait! The bad news about denial isn't over yet. There is another reason why denying your cravings leads to weight gain. As you try to resist and achieve victory by not giving in to the craving, you start recruiting other foods to assist you in the battle. Before conceding defeat to your desired food, you end up eating at least four other foods first. I call it "eating around the craving." Let me explain.

If, right now, you are yearning for something sweet, but vow to have the willpower to abstain, you will soon start grazing the cupboards and refrigerator in search of satisfaction. Maybe you have some carrot sticks, then an apple, then some nonfat cottage cheese, then some rice cakes. But do you feel satisfied? No. Two hours later, you're still not satisfied and can't resist any longer—so you finally give in and eat six cookies. No wonder we think that food cravings cause weight gain; first we eat around the craving, and then we end up overeating the desired food anyway.

•

Eating Around the Craving		Immediately Satisfying the Craving	
carrot sticks	25 calories	2 cookies	200 calories
apple	80 calories		
cottage cheese	100 calories		
rice cakes	50 calories		
6 cookies	600 calories		
Total	**855 calories**	**Total**	**200 calories**

Consuming 855 calories means that weight gain is inevitable, while it is highly unlikely with 200 calories. Fulfilling your food cravings will not lead to weight gain if you listen to your body and give it the small amount that it needs. It's a medical fact that women are extremely efficient at storing calories in their fat cells; but that efficiency kicks into gear only when you eat more than your body needs to function over the next few hours. If you respond to your food cravings by eating a small amount when you are *hungry*, your body and brain will use it before your fat cells have any idea what's going on.

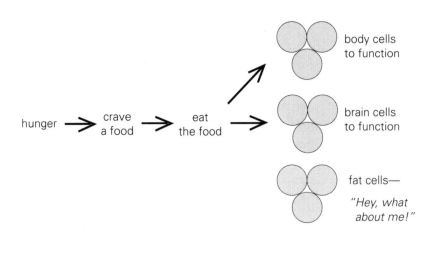

hunger → crave a food → eat the food →

body cells to function

brain cells to function

fat cells— *"Hey, what about me!"*

•

Eat a small amount of what you want when you are hungry—and you will *not* gain weight. Here's one last supporting argument to convince you of this concept. Think of someone you know who is a naturally thin person. Denise immediately thought of her sister. "She eats what she wants when she wants it. Sometimes it's ice cream and other times it's carrot sticks—but it's always about a handful of food. She's never had a weight problem while I've been struggling with my weight for the past 15 years."

After Denise and I spent a few sessions on trust, hunger, and food cravings, she finally held the belief that listening to your body will lead to weight loss instead of weight gain (and, as a result, she ultimately lost forty-two pounds!). But then her next food-craving fear surfaced: "Okay, if I satisfy my food cravings, I won't gain weight and will actually lose weight, but my diet will be unhealthy."

YOUR DIET WILL *NOT* BE UNHEALTHY

First of all, eating a cookie or a piece of chocolate or a scoop of ice cream does not make your diet unhealthy. Eating a moderate amount of sugar and fat fits within the context of a healthy diet. Second, female food cravings are not limited to high-fat and high-sugar foods. If permitted, a woman's body will guide her to the most optimal diet for mind and body—and that includes a wide variety of foods, from chocolate to chicken to cabbage. Those women who are in tune with their bodies and regularly fulfill their food cravings are more likely to have a variety of food messages. They still crave chocolate and caramel sometimes, but they also crave breads, cereals, crackers, fruits, and vegetables.

If you listen to your body and respond to its needs, your diet may very well increase in its nutritional quality.

•

By learning to trust your body, you will find that you often desire the foods containing the nutrients your body needs.

- If your body needs vitamin C, you may crave oranges.
- If your body needs magnesium, you may crave spinach.
- If your body needs beta-carotene, you may crave carrots.
- If your body needs iron, you may crave red meat.
- If your body needs calcium, you may crave milk.
- if your body needs salt, you may crave pickles.

When you trust and listen to your body, it will begin to request the foods that are packed with the specific nutrient it needs. This is not a new concept. Some of the most interesting food-craving studies have been done with children and pregnant women. If offered a wide variety of foods, young children will choose the right combination of foods to provide the vitamins and minerals their bodies need. Food cravings are extremely common during pregnancy, and even the most bizarre of them have a biological rationale. We've all heard of and maybe experienced the pickles-and-ice-cream phenomenon. The calcium, sugar, and fat in the ice cream and the salt in the pickles provide a combination needed during pregnancy. Even *pica*, or cravings for nonfood items such as clay, dirt, and chalk, can be explained as an adaptive response to provide nutrients; they have a mineral content equivalent to prenatal vitamins. In Thailand, pregnant women have been documented eating rotting wood. It took a while to figure out why, but the bacteria decomposing the wood provided the B vitamins lacking in their diet.

What nutrient-packed foods (other than rotting wood) have you experienced cravings for? Think of fruits, vegetables, grains, milk products, and protein foods. Take a moment and write them down.

•

_____   _____   _____
_____   _____   _____
_____   _____   _____
_____   _____   _____
_____   _____   _____
_____   _____   _____

Whatever foods you listed, I'm confident that I could find some nutritional, biological explanation for the craving.

Julie wanted an explanation for her occasional intense desire for kiwi fruit. When I told her that the potassium content of kiwi was higher than that of most other foods, she understood that her body was probably low in potassium and needed the kiwi. Satisfied with the kiwi-potassium rationale, she then wanted an explanation for the raw oyster craving that she got once a month. Although she expected to hear something about oysters being an aphrodisiac, discovering that two oysters provide the daily recommended allowance for zinc made more sense.

If your nutrient-packed food craving list was blank, come back to it after completing the five steps of the **ON** Plan. As you encourage and permit your body to send you messages, you'll become aware of all of your varied food needs.

"Why can't I force my body to demand only the healthy nutrient-packed foods? I'm craving more fruits, vegetables, and grains, but I still want a chocolate chip cookie every day."

Since when did eating a chocolate chip cookie label your diet as unhealthy? The answer is, since we started to categorize foods as "healthy" and "unhealthy" and have been led to believe that eating an "unhealthy" food makes for an unhealthy diet.

First of all, no single food determines the nutritional quality of your diet. And second, some of the foods you consider

•

unhealthy may not be. I'd like to use an activity to reprogram your healthy-vs.-unhealthy food mentality. Go through the following list and rate each food as healthy or unhealthy with a short explanation for your rating.

	Healthy?	Unhealthy?	Why?
chocolate	_____	_____	_____
carob	_____	_____	_____
ice cream	_____	_____	_____
nonfat frozen yogurt	_____	_____	_____
pasta	_____	_____	_____
hamburger	_____	_____	_____
french fries	_____	_____	_____
baked potato	_____	_____	_____
nonfat milk	_____	_____	_____
whole milk	_____	_____	_____
carrots	_____	_____	_____
bananas	_____	_____	_____
bagel	_____	_____	_____
bran muffin	_____	_____	_____
granola	_____	_____	_____
pretzels	_____	_____	_____
shrimp	_____	_____	_____
tofu	_____	_____	_____
margarine	_____	_____	_____
butter	_____	_____	_____
mayonnaise	_____	_____	_____
cholesterol-free mayonnaise	_____	_____	_____

This list was probably fairly easy to do since the good food/bad food debate has been going on for a decade or more,

•

and any food that contains fat, sugar, or salt is considered hands-down bad.

But did you know that all of the foods you rated as healthy can easily and quickly become unhealthy? Most people rate pasta as healthy; it's nonfat, cholesterol-free, and sugar-free. However, for some reason we think that pasta must be heaped on our plates in mountainous quantities (not to mention the parmesan cheese on top and garlic bread on the side). Like any food, pasta becomes unhealthy when you overeat it. The first cup of pasta your body needed, but the second (and third?) cup was converted to fat and stored as fat. A cup of pasta is a healthy choice; a pound of pasta is an unhealthy choice.

I could go through the same explanation with every single food you labeled as healthy—nonfat milk, bagels, pretzels, etc. Overeating transforms them into an unhealthy food. Fat is the storage form of any food. Even if the food contains no fat at all, when you are eating more of it than your body needs, it is converted to fat and stored as fat. You end up feeding your fat cells, not your body and brain.

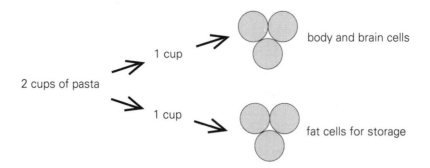

In addition, there are some so-called healthy foods that don't deserve their "100 percent stamp of approval" rating. Tofu is one of them. It was designated as one of the first

•

"health foods" because it's a vegetable protein without cholesterol or saturated fat, but—tofu is still high in fat with 50 percent of its calories derived from unsaturated fats. Two more examples: margarine and cholesterol-free mayonnaise. Both contain no cholesterol but are 100 percent fat.

Now let's look at a food you rated as unhealthy. Most people rate french fries as unhealthy because they are deep-fried. It may be difficult to convince you that french fries can be a healthy choice, but let me give it a try. If you biologically crave them, you probably need the fat or the combination of salt, fat, and starch, and if you eat a handful when you are hungry, they will be burned by your body for all of its functions—not stored in your fat cells and not embedded in your arteries.

A small amount of any food is healthy; a large amount of any food is unhealthy.

"So what you are telling me is that any food is okay in moderation. I'm sick and tired of hearing the word *moderation*. The only thing I practice in moderation *is* moderation." Yes, it is the "moderation is the key to health" theory but from a different perspective. This time it's moderation as defined by your body's needs and moderation in all foods, whether they are labeled as healthy or unhealthy.

Actually, the whole definition of healthy eating is relative. It depends on our culture, beliefs, and food availability. In impoverished countries, every food is considered healthy because it will help to sustain life. In other parts of the world, foods we would never think of eating are considered healthy. For example, cockroaches are frequently found on the dinner plate in Sri Lanka, and bees are eaten in certain sections of China. You may not consider cockroaches and bees a healthy addition to your diet, but the Sri Lankans and Chinese do.

•

I hope that I have been successful in realistically transforming these three food-craving fears into three food-craving revelations: You *can* stop, you will *not* gain weight, and your diet will *not* be unhealthy! Now let's transform uncertainty into confidence.

YOU *CAN* IDENTIFY A BIOLOGICAL FOOD CRAVING

Before you can fully trust your female food cravings, you need to be able to differentiate between a biological food craving and an emotional food craving.

Many women ask me:

"How can I be sure that it is a biological craving? What if it is an emotional craving? How can I tell the difference?"

The major difference is that biological cravings are based on your *body's* needs, and emotional cravings are based on your *heart's* needs—but sometimes that knowledge is not quite enough.

You can use a variety of techniques to distinguish between a biological and an emotional food craving. One of your best tools is *hunger*. **Hunger always precedes biological food cravings.**

It's a biological craving if:

- you *are* physiologically hungry
- it doesn't go away if you try to wait it out
- it intensifies over time
- nothing will satisfy the craving except the craved food

•

In contrast, it's an emotional craving if:

- you are *not* physiologically hungry
- it does go away if you try to wait it out
- the craving does not intensify over time, but the emotion does
- doing something else will satisfy the real need and the craving will disappear

Being aware of your physiological hunger signals will give you the confidence to satisfy your female food cravings. However, just as food cravings are foreign and frightening to some women because they have denied them for so long, so are hunger signals. Hunger is a natural, internal message that we have tried to ignore, fight, and override. We've been told to deny hunger, don't give in, wait until you are extremely hungry before you eat, don't trust your hunger.

Well, hunger is definitely on your side. When you are hungry, you need food and the cravings surface for the specific foods you need. When you then eat the food and are completely satisfied, you feel great and are no longer hungry.

What are your physiological signals of hunger?

Knowing your specific hunger signals is vital to the success of the **ON** Plan. Hunger signals can come from your stomach as it informs you that it is empty or from your brain as it informs you that it is lacking in energy supply.

Stomach Signals	Brain Signals
growls	fogginess
pangs	lack of concentration
hollow feeling	headache
empty feeling	fatigue

•

"I don't think my body transmits any hunger signals. I'm not sure that I have ever felt hungry." Jessica was concerned that her hunger signals were nonexistent. They were there; it's just that she had been ignoring her hunger signals for so long that they gave up due to lack of attention. When she started paying attention, they started signaling.

To help you get acquainted with your body's hunger signals, let me introduce you to the Hunger/Fullness Rating Scale.

THE HUNGER/FULLNESS RATING SCALE

10—absolutely, positively, lie-on-the-floor stuffed
9—so full that it is starting to hurt
8—very full and bloated
7—starting to feel uncomfortable
6—slightly overeating
5—perfectly comfortable
4—first signals that it's time to eat
3—strong signals to eat
2—very hungry, irritable
1—extreme hunger, dizziness

If you are at level 5 or above, you are not hungry and, therefore, your body and brain don't need anything. If you are craving something, it is not biological—it's emotional. Satisfy your real emotional need by taking care of yourself in some other, more effective way. Ask yourself what you really need: To talk to a friend? To punch a pillow? To take a bath?

If you are at level 3 or 4, your body is telling you that it needs some food, and your cravings are telling you the specific foods that it needs. This *is* a biological female food craving.

If you are at level 1 or 2, your body is too hungry, and

•

although you may be biologically craving something, you'll most likely end up overeating it, fearing weight gain, and then start depriving yourself again.

Hunger *always* precedes biological food cravings, but not emotional food cravings. There is another technique to help you distinguish between body hunger and heart hunger: **Negative mood also precedes biological food cravings and improved mood is the result of fulfilling the craving.**

When biological food cravings are the product of your brain requesting assistance in elevating a pleasurable brain chemical (which is often the case), then you may feel sad, stressed, tired, anxious, or angry. And—eating the food will make you feel better.

When you experience an emotional craving, you may also feel sad, stressed, tired, anxious, or angry—or all of the above—but the similarity stops there. After eating the craved food, you will not feel better and may very well feel worse. Your real needs weren't addressed, so the depression or anger or other feeling persists and intensifies.

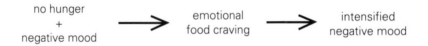

To differentiate between biological and emotional food cravings, awareness of your mood states is just as important as awareness of your hunger levels. This recognition may be more difficult than you think. When you are asked, "How do you feel?" how do you usually respond? Most people respond with either "Okay" or "Fine." Too often, these replies don't reflect your feelings, but are just easy answers.

•

To help you identify your specific feelings and moods, I am going to ask you to rephrase the question "How do I feel?" to *"What* am I feeling?" Use the following list of ten moods to specifically answer the question. For each of the five more negative moods, five positive are listed. Biological food cravings are often preceded by negative moods, but so are emotional food cravings. The difference is that biological cravings are also preceded by hunger, and after eating the craved food, moods improve.

MOOD SCALE

Negative Moods	Positive Moods
sad	happy
angry	content
anxious	calm
stressed	relaxed
tired	energetic

So, whenever you are not quite sure whether the craving is emotional or biological, you now have two tools: the hunger scale and the mood scale. Use them and ask yourself some important questions:

> Am I hungry?
> What am I feeling?
> Will food really help?
> What do I really need?

Creating a short delay may also help you to identify what is really going on. Use the *fifteen-minute test:* Drink a glass of water and wait fifteen minutes, then ask yourself the above questions. If you are hungry and the craving is still there, most likely it's biological.

Many women eat for emotional reasons from time to time, and for some women it may be daily. If these techniques

•

don't help and you know that you are an emotional eater, I strongly advise that you seek professional guidance from a licensed therapist. You'll continue using food for emotional nourishment until you no longer need to. If your depression is due to a divorce, if your anxiety is due to a layoff, if your fatigue is due to an eighty-hour work week—then you need to deal with the source of those feelings.

You *can* trust your female food cravings when you are *hungry* and when you have identified your *feelings*.

STOP! ARE YOU EXPERIENCING A FEMALE FOOD CRAVING RIGHT NOW?

If you are and you are also hungry, put down this book, satisfy your food craving, and come back with renewed spirit.

Every now and then throughout the book, I will ask you to stop reading, pause a moment, and check in with your female food cravings. I want you to get in the habit of acknowledging and responding to your instinctive food needs.

Now that you have all the knowledge and skills to trust your female food cravings, let's put this first step into practice.

•

WEEK 1:   Your **ON** Action Plan

STEP 1:   Trust Your Female Food Cravings

GOALS:
1. Identify and overcome your food craving fears.
2. Become aware of your hunger signals and mood states.
3. Distinguish between a biological and an emotional craving.
4. Begin responding to your female food cravings.

TECHNIQUES:
1. Identify the reasons why you overeat and fear weight gain.
2. Immediately satisfy your food cravings with small amounts.
3. Try the morning experiment.
4. Don't eat around the craving.
5. Acknowledge that you also crave fruits, vegetables, grains, milk products, and protein foods.
6. Reevaluate your definition of a healthy diet.
7. Put your craving to the 15-minute test.
8. Ask yourself, "Am I hungry? What am I feeling? "What do I really need?"
9. Use the Hunger/Fullness Rating Scale.
10. Use the Mood Scale.
11. Keep eating records for the next week to practice these techniques.

•

After each chapter, I'll going to ask you to stop for a week and focus on the specific step of the **ON** Plan. Some of you may be tempted to read straight through the entire book. If that's the case, come back to this page again and really begin the program.

I'm also going to strongly encourage some record keeping, but not the typical food records where you have to write down exact amounts and count up the calories. There is no calorie counting in this plan! These are *eating records* that will encourage you to eat what you are craving and help you gain an awareness of all your food needs.

For this first week of the **ON** Plan, the goal is to help you gain the trust and confidence in your biological female food cravings. The only focus will be on checking in with your body to allow it to tell you if it is craving any particular food, if it is hungry (because hunger always accompanies biological food cravings), and how it is feeling. I'm not really concerned about what foods you're craving or even how much you ate— just the messages from your body.

On the following pages are a sample eating record and a blank record for the first step of the **ON** Plan. Every hour, record the awareness of a food craving, your hunger level, your mood state, and then determine whether or not it is a biological craving. If it's biological, don't hesitate to satisfy it!

It's possible to be hungry and not crave a particular food. Sometimes your body just wants calories and is indifferent to the source of those calories. Biological food cravings surface only when your body and/or brain need something. Even if a day or more goes by without a food craving—don't be concerned. With practice, you'll become a master at the art of listening to your body.

•

EATING RECORDS FOR TRUSTING
YOUR FEMALE FOOD CRAVINGS

Time	Food Craving	Hunger Level	Mood State	Biological or Emotional?	Did You Satisfy It?
6:00 am	no				
7:00 am	bagel	4	tired	biological	yes!
8:00 am	no				
9:00 am	no				
10:00 am	crackers	3	anxious	biological	yes - felt better
11:00 am	no				
12:00 pm	don't think so				
1:00 pm	salad	3	ok	biological	yes - needed greens!
2:00 pm	no				
3:00 pm	candy bar	5	stressed	emotional	yes - couldn't help it
4:00 pm	chocolate	6	stressed!	emotional	NO!
5:00 pm	no				
6:00 pm	no				
7:00 pm	chicken	3	content	biological	yes
8:00 pm	no				
9:00 pm	no				

•

EATING RECORDS FOR TRUSTING
YOUR FEMALE FOOD CRAVINGS

Time	Food Craving	Hunger Level	Mood State	Biological or Emotional?	Did You Satisfy It?
——	——	——	——	——	——
——	——	——	——	——	——
——	——	——	——	——	——
——	——	——	——	——	——
——	——	——	——	——	——
——	——	——	——	——	——
——	——	——	——	——	——
——	——	——	——	——	——
——	——	——	——	——	——
——	——	——	——	——	——
——	——	——	——	——	——
——	——	——	——	——	——
——	——	——	——	——	——
——	——	——	——	——	——
——	——	——	——	——	——
——	——	——	——	——	——
——	——	——	——	——	——
——	——	——	——	——	——
——	——	——	——	——	——
——	——	——	——	——	——
——	——	——	——	——	——
——	——	——	——	——	——
——	——	——	——	——	——
——	——	——	——	——	——
——	——	——	——	——	——

•

Five

I ALWAYS THOUGHT THAT FOODS loaded with sugar gave my moods and energy the biggest boost, but now I realize that any benefits from sugar don't last very long, and it's the high-starch foods that keep me in tip-top shape for the longest period of time. I used to crave candy, soft drinks, and desserts, but since I started trusting and listening to my food needs, breads and pasta are at the top of my female pleasure food list."

I hope that you will all come to the same realization that Jessica did. Your female food cravings are your female pleasure foods. They pleasure your body and mind by making you feel as good and function as well as you possibly can. And, because the high-starch foods (and chocolate!) keep your brain in a constant state of contentment, it would choose them the majority of the time. It may take you a while before your brain and body let you know what their top female plea-

•

sure foods are, but this next step of the **ON** Plan will help them voice their strong opinions.

What you crave is a reflection of what you need, what will make you feel good—and what you personally crave may be very different from what I or what your friends crave. Because of these individual differences, I can't give you a complete list of the female pleasure foods; you have to devise your own list.

Your female pleasure foods are influenced by food availability, food preferences, childhood experiences, taste buds, metabolism, and biochemistry. Hormonal levels also greatly influence the foods that you crave. What you hunger for ten days before your period may be very different from what you crave a day before your period. Your food demands as a postmenopausal woman may be different from those you experienced as a premenopausal woman.

I'm sure that you could list some of your female pleasure foods this very moment, but in reading this chapter, I hope you come to some new awarenesses and a few surprises.

You will always crave chocolate sometimes (often? always?), sugar sometimes, fat sometimes, salt sometimes—but if you are truly listening to your body, you'll crave starch the majority of the time. Why? Because starch is your brain's longtime companion.

STARCH: YOUR BRAIN'S LONGTIME COMPANION

If women had only known the immense benefits of starch on both the body and brain, we would never have reduced our intake by 25 percent over the last fifty years. We wouldn't have ordered the diet dinner plates with cottage cheese, a hamburger patty, and no bun. We would never have followed

•

the numerous low-carbohydrate weight loss diets. No wonder the number-one complaint on those diets was irritability; the carbohydrate content was too low for a serotonin release, and the brain was deprived of calming chemicals.

You don't need to restrict starches any longer. They are not an enemy—but rather a strong ally that stabilizes your mood and energy while also providing exceptional taste and satisfaction.

In my workshops, I often get the question, "What's the difference between starch and complex carbohydrates?" There is no difference; both terms are used to categorize grain products, which are made up of hundreds of glucose molecules attached to each other. Whether it's bread, crackers, cereal, pasta, rice, pretzels, or potatoes—chemically they all look something like this (G=Glucose):

G – G – G – G – G – G – G – G – G – G – G – G

In order for starches to be digested, they must be broken down with the digestive enzymes into more simple molecules. First, there is an enzyme responsible for breaking the complex carbohydrate in half.

G – G – G – G – G – G **/** G – G – G – G – G – G

Next, another enzyme is responsible for breaking it in half again.

G – G – G **/** G – G – G **/** G – G – G **/** G – G – G

•

And so on. Until eventually the long, complex starch molecule is broken down to simple, single glucose molecules that are ready to be absorbed into your bloodstream.

bloodstream

This entire digestive process for starch takes time, and within about two hours, all of the starch has been broken down to glucose and absorbed into your bloodstream. Over that two-hour time period, both your blood glucose and your blood insulin are rising. Insulin is the hormone responsible for transporting the glucose from the bloodstream into the cells. Every cell requires glucose to function, but your brain cells must have a constant source of glucose and thus appear to have the highest requirement.

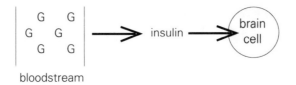

bloodstream

The slow and steady effects of starch maintain a constant source of energy to the brain. Your brain is getting what it needs to function efficiently; it's quite pleased with your starch choice and lets you know by maximizing your energy level, productivity, and concentration.

•

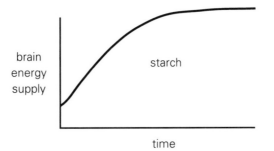

Your brain is also appreciative for the long-term effects of starch on brain serotonin levels. The digestion of starch allows for the building blocks of serotonin to enter the brain at the perfect pace and keep serotonin production going, and going, and going. The result is that you feel calm, relaxed, and at peace for hours.

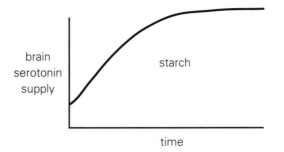

Starches are not fattening (unless you overeat them); they are your brain's longtime companion because of the sustained benefits on brain energy *and* brain serotonin levels.

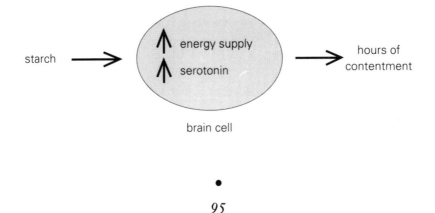

•

There is one more benefit from starch cravings. If you exercise regularly, your body's friendship with starch grows even closer. Starch will replenish the glucose stores in your muscle and liver (called glycogen stores) that were mobilized during your walk, or bike ride, or aerobics class. Fulfilling your starch cravings will give you additional energy during your workouts.

No matter how you look at it—workout energy, brain energy, or mood stability—starch provides the super premium high-octane fuel for your body. We put the highest-quality gas in our cars, why wouldn't we put the highest-quality fuel in our bodies? Starch will keep your body's engine clean and take the knocks and pings out of your brain.

Which of the high-starch foods are your female pleasure foods?

With the following list of complex carbohydrates, you will begin to identify your female pleasure foods. Female pleasure foods have three characteristics.

1. They are the foods you like, that taste good to you, and that are satisfying.
2. They are the foods you crave when you are hungry and when your mood needs a lift.
3. They are the foods that revitalize your moods, energy, and body.

You will assess these three characteristics by rating your starch preferences, how often you crave them, how often you eat them, and how they make you feel.

How often do you crave high-starch foods that you dislike? Probably never. These are not your female pleasure foods.

How often do you crave high-starch foods that you feel

•

Food	Do You Like It? (like, dislike, neutral)	Do You Crave It? (never, sometimes, often)	Do You Eat It? (never, sometimes, often)	How Do You Feel After Eating?
whole-grain bread				
white bread				
pita bread				
rolls				
bagels				
English muffins				
bran muffins				
blueberry muffins				
corn bread				
sourdough bread				
French baguettes				
croissants				
popovers				
stuffing				
bread sticks				
crackers				
rice cakes				
pretzels				
popcorn				
corn				
potatoes				
white rice				
brown rice				
rice pilaf				
pasta				
cold cereal				
hot cereal				

●

neutral about? Not very often. It's unlikely that these are your female pleasure foods.

How often do you crave high-starch foods that you like and that make you feel good? Just about all the time. **These are your female pleasure foods.** Go back to the list and circle all of your high-starch female pleasure foods.

Now for the interesting question: How often do you *eat* the foods that you like, you crave, and make you feel good?

- If you've been denying and dieting, probably seldom.
- If you've just begun trusting and listening to your female food needs, maybe it's sometimes.
- After you've finished the **ON** Plan, I hope the answer will consistently be often.

Another question may be coming to mind: If starch is the top female pleasure food and my brain's longtime companion, then why do I crave sugar at all? A number of possible explanations are:

- You have not been taking advantage of the brain benefits of starch and need a quick fix (when you start eating more starch, you'll find that you crave sugar less).
- Hormonal fluctuations premenstrually or during menopause have caused brain serotonin levels to drop quickly and your brain demands sugar.
- You are overhungry and blood glucose is low.
- Your brain is responding to quick changes in mood and craves sugar for self-medication.
- The triple-chocolate fudge layer cake looks so damn good that you just gotta have it whether or not your brain needs it (we can't underestimate the power of the taste buds urging us on every now and then).

•

Sugar produces the same physiological changes as starch, but on a different time schedule. Instead of a longtime companion, sugar is more like a short-lived romance.

SUGAR: A BITTERSWEET RELATIONSHIP

The sweet part about sugar is that it does quickly boost blood sugar and serotonin levels, and is like a first aid kit for the brain in an emergency. The bitter part is that sugar only temporarily mends the brain, and the boost is followed by a bust in which blood sugar levels plummet.

Just as the term starch is interchangeable with complex carbohydrates, so too is sugar with simple carbohydrates. The terms are actually quite descriptive. Complex carbohydrates are long, more complicated chains of glucose molecules, and, as you've probably already guessed, simple carbohydrates are very short chains of glucose molecules—only two per chain.

G – G

Simple carbohydrates are simple to eat, simple to digest, and simple to absorb. The first, middle, and last step in the digestive process is to break the molecule in half. Only one enzyme is needed, and *voilà*, you have single glucose molecules ready to be quickly absorbed into your bloodstream.

G / G

↓↓

bloodstream

This digestive process is so simple that it takes almost no time at all. Within minutes, your blood glucose is on the rise,

•

and your brain is bombarded with energy molecules. Sounds pretty good; however, any positive brain benefits are short-lived and are usually followed by a significant drop in energy and mood.

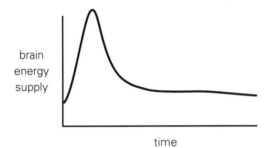

Within thirty minutes of eating the sweet, you may feel tired, irritable, and lethargic. In fact, you feel lower after eating the sugar than before you ate it. And you are most likely going to crave sugar again soon because your brain is in need of a quick pick-me-up. This is one of the biological explanations for why once you start eating sugar, you can't seem to stop. The brain feels like it's on a roller coaster with the sugar highs and sugar lows. Your moods, energy, and productivity are strapped in the backseat of the roller coaster dipping, climbing, and whipping around the curves with centrifugal force.

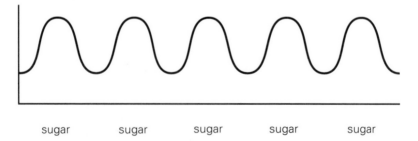

Which would you choose? The quick sugar power burst or the slow, steady starch benefit? Think of the tale of the

•

tortoise and the hare and remember, it's the slow and steady that wins the race. With sugar, your brain is ecstatic for about twenty minutes and then poops out; with starch, your brain is content for hours.

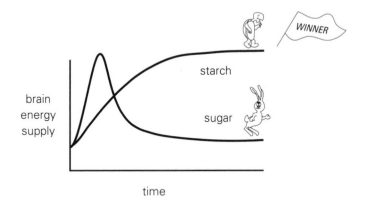

"Why can't I have both?" Liz's mind was working overtime. "What if I ate some jelly beans with a rice cake? Wouldn't I then get both the immediate sugar burst and the long-term starch benefit?" Liz was right. Especially if you are craving sugar, make sure you have a rice cake or some other starch with the sugar food to prevent the bitter/sweet effects and receive the sustained benefit of starch at the same time.

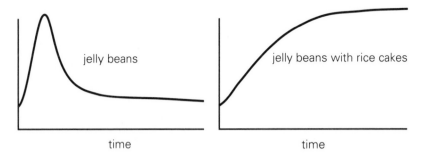

If you have a craving for sugar, fulfill it—just make sure you have a small amount of starch with it to make the roller coaster ride more like one on a Ferris wheel.

•

"So what's the best sugar choice and what's the best starch choice?" asked Liz, looking for specifics. There is no "best"; it's whatever you prefer and crave. All starches are created equal and all sugars are created equal. Honey, fruit sugar, table sugar, and processed sugar are all digested and absorbed in the same way. And, once they enter your blood as glucose, your brain doesn't know the difference. It knows only that it's getting the glucose and serotonin it needs. With some new information surfacing on the glycemic index of foods (the effect of food on blood glucose), don't be too alarmed if you hear that potatoes raise blood glucose more than candy or bread more than fruit. This information is most important for diabetics, who after years of sugar restriction, can now enjoy some sweets in moderation. More proof that sugar is not a forbidden food!

Which sugar foods are your female pleasure foods?

To help you identify your female pleasure foods in the sugar category, here is another food list to rate your preferences, how often you crave them, how often you eat them, and how they make you feel.

How often do you crave high-sugar foods that you dislike? (Assuming that you dislike any at all.)

How often do you crave high-sugar foods that you feel neutral about? Again, probably not very often.

How often do you crave high-sugar foods that you like and that make you feel good? **These are your female pleasure foods.** Go back and circle these sugar pleasure foods.

How often do you *eat* foods that you like, you crave, and make you feel the best? With the **ON** Plan working in your favor, hopefully you will eat them—and add a small amount of starch.

Many of the sugar foods we crave are not 100 percent sugar. They have something else added to them that enhances

•

Food	Do You Like It? (like, dislike, neutral)	Do You Crave It? (never, sometimes, often)	Do You Eat It? (never, sometimes, often)	How Do You Feel After Eating?
apples				
oranges				
bananas				
pears				
grapefruit				
melon				
strawberries				
blueberries				
raspberries				
raisins				
prunes				
dried apricots				
orange juice				
apple juice				
pineapple juice				
hard candies				
lollipops				
caramel				
licorice				
marshmallows				
jelly beans				
Jell-O				
Popsicles				
regular soft drinks				
table sugar				
cookies				
donuts				
pastries				
ice cream				
frozen yogurt				
ice milk				
sherbet				
sorbet				

the flavor and smooths the consistency. That added component is fat. Still under debate is the question: Are we craving the sugar or the fat or the blend of sugar and fat? Based on a woman's changing hormones and biochemistry, it could be any possibility because fat is just as close a friend as sugar, and like sugar, once you invite it into your diet, it can overstay its welcome.

FAT: THE FRIEND THAT WOULDN'T LEAVE

Fat is like one of those houseguests who won't leave no matter how many hints you give. Spending a little bit of time together can be enjoyable, but with too much time, you are sick of their company. Some fat, especially at the right times, can be an enjoyable eating companion, but too much fat can take its toll and make you sick.

A moderate amount of fat is a friend to a woman's body and mind because:

1. It is a female food craving and female pleasure food.
2. It keeps our brain cells happy with endorphins.
3. It keeps our skin healthy with essential fatty acids and fat-soluble vitamins.
4. It keeps our fat cells happy with ready-to-store calories.

"Why on earth would I ever want to make my fat cells happy?" Janet couldn't understand why she would want to be friendly and amenable to her fat cells. Her goal had always been to starve them to death and bury them in the "Tomb of the Unknown Fat Cells." But, if you don't at least minimally please your fat cells, they will get angry and retaliate by becoming more efficient in storing and growing.

Some fat is a female friend, but there is a fine line beyond which that friend becomes not so friendly. If our diets are

•

high in fat, it will make our hips and thighs bigger than we would like, increase our risk of disease, and give us a fat hangover.

"A fat hangover? That's a great term for it because I know exactly what you are talking about. You wake up groggy, puffy, and you feel like you consumed a bottle of wine instead of a package of cookies." The hangover feeling is due to your body trying to metabolize the fat globules bombarding your bloodstream.

Fat in moderation is a friend—not too much and not too little. Unless you've been trying to eliminate fat from your diet, you probably don't have the problem of eating too little fat. However, with the latest race to cut fat lower and lower, some women are trying to eat "fat-free," convinced that it is the secret to weight loss, beating the odds of breast cancer, and warding off heart disease.

Eating a fat-free diet is not the secret to the fountain of youth nor the prevention of disease. Many risk factors and variables affect our health. And too little fat can present some problems for women.

Not too long ago, Belinda made an appointment with me to discuss what she called her "fat dilemma." She and her husband had been following a virtually no-fat diet for the previous six weeks. "He feels absolutely great, wakes up turbo-energy-charged every morning, has lost fourteen pounds, and has become a food fanatic. My experience with this so-called healthy eating plan couldn't be more different. I'm irritable, my skin is dry and flaky, I can't wake up in the morning, I'm tired all day long—and I've gained four pounds! Go figure. I can't take it any longer. I'm craving some high-fat foods that I've never craved before and am about to consider an all out fat binge. What's the matter with me? Do I lack discipline? Do I need to restrict my fat intake even more?"

If you have tried to follow the latest fat-free trend, you

•

may have had similar experiences to Belinda's. As it turned out, nothing at all was the matter with her, and she wasn't lacking anything except the proper food for her body and brain to function efficiently. Too little fat perturbs our fat cells and triggers the starvation response to conserve fat for pregnancy and breast-feeding. Men's fat cells are so good-natured that they can follow a very low-fat diet and reap the benefits. When we try to do the same, our bodies quickly inform us that we are on the wrong track.

Will your body also inform you if you are eating too much fat? You may experience the fat hangover, but after a while you get accustomed to it, and the low-energy, bogged-down feeling starts to feel normal. High blood cholesterol is a sign of too much fat, but you won't know about it unless you have your blood cholesterol checked. Weight gain is probably the most obvious sign of too much fat, but you may blame it on your genes, age, or slow metabolism—and not acknowledge the strong cause-and-effect relationship. **A high-fat diet leads to a high-fat body.**

The typical American woman is consuming a high-fat diet, with 37 percent of her calories every day coming from fat. Are you a typical American woman? If you are, then you are eating more fat than your female body and brain need to function efficiently.

> too much fat: more than 30% of total calories
> too little fat: less than 20% of total calories
> fat-friendly: 20–30% of total calories

If you trust and respond to your eating instincts, you will naturally eat fat-friendly—20 to 30 percent of your calories from fat is enough to keep your moods elevated with brain chemicals, keep your skin healthy with fatty acids and fat-soluble vitamins, and keep your fat cells content with just

•

enough fat to prevent the starvation response without triggering weight gain. By eating fat-friendly, you get all of the benefits without any of the repercussions of deprivation.

"Is there a 'good' type of fat for my brain like there is for my heart?" Terri had been buying olive oil by the gallon container thinking that she was benefiting her heart. Using olive oil instead of butter may be better for your heart, but using a lot of olive oil isn't good for your heart or any other organ in your body, including your brain. Too much vegetable fat will give you just as much of a fat hangover as too much animal fat.

Whatever the type of fat, it's usually eaten in combination with something else that your body may or may not need. If you are craving french fries, maybe it's the fat your body needs, maybe it's the starch—or maybe it's the combination of both fat and starch. If you are craving a candy bar, maybe it's the fat, maybe the sugar—or again the combination. I did have a client once who craved pure butter. She would take a small chunk and eat it as a snack a couple of times a month. That turns my stomach instead of turning on my brain, but for her it worked.

Which high-fat foods are your female pleasure foods?

Answer that question by analyzing your fat preferences, how often you crave them, how often you eat them, and how they make you feel. I could have gone on and on with this list, but the foods I choose to include range from 50 percent to 100 percent of the calories derived from fat.

How often do you crave high-fat foods you dislike?

How often do you crave high-fat foods you feel neutral about?

How often do you crave high-fat foods that you like and make you feel good? **These are your female pleasure foods.** Go back to the list and circle all of your high-fat female pleasure foods.

•

Food	Do You Like It? (like, dislike, neutral)	Do You Crave It? (never, sometimes, often)	Do You Eat It? (never, sometimes, often)	How Do You Feel After Eating?
butter	_____	_____	_____	_____
margarine	_____	_____	_____	_____
sour cream	_____	_____	_____	_____
whipped cream	_____	_____	_____	_____
cream cheese	_____	_____	_____	_____
salad dressing	_____	_____	_____	_____
olive oil	_____	_____	_____	_____
corn oil	_____	_____	_____	_____
canola oil	_____	_____	_____	_____
safflower oil	_____	_____	_____	_____
peanut oil	_____	_____	_____	_____
shortening	_____	_____	_____	_____
lard	_____	_____	_____	_____
avocado	_____	_____	_____	_____
french fries	_____	_____	_____	_____
snack chips	_____	_____	_____	_____
candy bars	_____	_____	_____	_____
donuts	_____	_____	_____	_____
croissants	_____	_____	_____	_____
cheese	_____	_____	_____	_____
cheesecake	_____	_____	_____	_____
pies	_____	_____	_____	_____
peanuts	_____	_____	_____	_____
peanut butter	_____	_____	_____	_____
bacon	_____	_____	_____	_____
sausage	_____	_____	_____	_____
deep-fried shrimp	_____	_____	_____	_____
deep-fried veggies	_____	_____	_____	_____

●

How often do you *eat* foods that you like, you crave, and make you feel good?

If you like, crave, and eat most foods in the high-fat food list, your diet could be high in fat. Have no fear! Right now, I just want you to become aware and to trust your body's messages. In the remaining chapters I will put on the finishing touches and help you to balance your fat intake and achieve a moderately low-fat diet.

You may be wondering why chocolate hasn't been included in any of these food lists yet. The reason is that I could have put chocolate in the sugar or the fat list, but I think it deserves a category of its own.

CHOCOLATE: OPTIMAL BRAIN HAPPINESS

Periodically over the years, consumers have lobbied for chocolate to have its own separate food group. This hasn't happened yet and most likely never will, but for the purpose of helping you to discover your female pleasure foods, I am giving chocolate the special attention it deserves by creating a separate category for it.

I realize that we have discussed the chemical composition of chocolate a number of times already, but let me briefly summarize it to emphasize its brain-pleasing qualities:

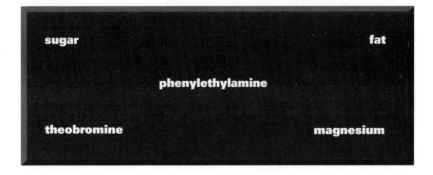

•

Chocolate is the only food that combines all of these ingredients, and probably some other brain-pleasing ones that haven't been discovered yet. Chocolate can cause a rush of both serotonin and endorphins into your brain cells and results in optimal brain happiness. With its remarkable effect on brain chemistry, it has been called the most effective non-drug antidepressant, "the ultimate de-PMS'er," and the "Prozac of plants." A pharmacist friend of mine came up with an idea for chocolate-covered Prozac. If he doesn't follow up on it, I'm sure that some other entrepreneur will.

If you already know that chocolate is not one of your female pleasure foods, then your body doesn't need it, and you can skip this section. Biochemically, we are all a bit different, or maybe your brain is already happy enough because you've been satisfying it with starches and a regular exercise program. For most of us, though, even if we eat starches and exercise regularly, chocolate cravings persist.

Through the years, I have asked thousands of men and women to describe their feelings toward chocolate. The gender differences speak for themselves.

The Men

- I could take it or leave it.
- It's okay.
- I really don't care for it.
- It's something to eat.
- Real men don't eat chocolate.
- Once in a while, I enjoy it.

The Women

- Pure ecstasy!
- It's deliciously divine.

●

- Heaven!
- A necessity of life
- It's cheaper than therapy.
- A chocolate chip cookie a day keeps the psychiatrist away.
- A warm fuzzy
- Woman does not live by bread alone, chocolate maybe.
- Life isn't worth living without chocolate.
- Unconditional love
- It makes me feel good all over.
- It's orgasmic.
- It's second only to sex.
- It's as good as sex.
- It's better than sex.

Since chocolate is often given a sexual connotation (I opted not to include some of the statements), I thought you might enjoy a PG-17 rated story that a client shared with me. She called it "The Birth of a Candy Bar."

Mr. Goodbar took *Bit-O-Honey* behind the *Powerhouse* on the corner of *Clark* and *Fifth Ave.* He made her *Tootsie Roll* as she felt transported to *Mars* and screamed, *"Oh! Henry!"* Soon she was a bit *Chunky* and nine months later had a *Baby Ruth.*

Is chocolate one of your female pleasure foods? An unnecessary question for the majority of us. Instead, what specific types of chocolate foods are your pleasure foods?

If you are a chocolate gourmand, it may be any and all. If you are a chocolate gourmet, it may be the highest quality only. To help you identify your female pleasure chocolate foods, here's another list to rate your preferences, how often you crave them, how often you eat them, and how they make you feel.

How often do you crave chocolate foods that you dislike? (If it is possible to dislike any chocolate food.)

•

Food	Do You Like It? (like, dislike, neutral)	Do You Crave It? (never, sometimes, often)	Do You Eat It? (never, sometimes, often)	How Do You Feel After Eating?
dark chocolate				
milk chocolate				
white chocolate				
chocolate candy				
chocolate ice cream				
chocolate yogurt				
chocolate mousse				
chocolate soufflé				
chocolate brownies				
chocolate cookies				
chocolate eclairs				
chocolate fudge				
chocolate truffles				
chocolate cake				
chocolate torte				
chocolate cream pie				
chocolate pudding				
chocolate fondue				
chocolate milk				
hot chocolate				

How often do you crave chocolate foods that you feel neutral about?

How often do you crave chocolate foods that you like and that make you feel good? **These are your female pleasure foods.** Go back and circle them in the list.

•

How often do you eat foods that you like, you crave, and make you feel good?

So far, starch and chocolate are tied for being a woman's best food friend. Sugar and fat can be reliable food friends too as long as we don't go overboard. There are two other female food friends to tell you about.

PROTEIN: AN OCCASIONAL COMRADE

As we've discussed, men prefer protein foods, especially meat, hot dogs, and eggs, and occasionally women prefer and crave protein, too. We don't, however, need as much protein as men because we have less testosterone and less muscle mass—but sometimes we will experience a fairly strong craving for protein—and only protein. If that is the case, listen to your body and respond to your needs.

Some women do report having protein cravings more frequently than cravings for carbohydrate, fat, or chocolate. "Does this mean that I have too much testosterone in my body?" asked Laura, a self-professed protein craver. Probably not; although all women have some testosterone in their bodies, craving protein does not mean that you have more testosterone or that your body is behaving more like a man's. Instead, it means that your body and brain need the protein to function at optimal capacity. It could be that your body is repairing damage or healing a wound. It could be that your body is building some muscle mass in response to your exercise program.

Another possibility is that your brain needs the protein to manufacture a certain brain chemical. Not serotonin and not the endorphins, but another brain chemical that we haven't discussed yet: dopamine. Although some of my clients think it will turn them into one of the seven dwarfs and make them

•

feel "dopey," dopamine does the opposite. It increases brain energy, alertness, and concentration.

When you eat foods high in protein, they are digested to amino acids, enter into your brain, and are converted to dopamine.

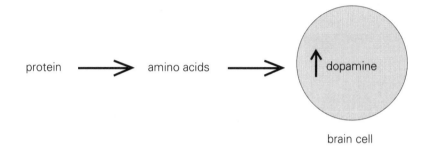

brain cell

"Why haven't you told me about this brain chemical?" asked Martina. "I could use all the alertness and concentration I can get." Because dopamine will give that boost in brain energy only if your gauge is reading Low, which doesn't happen very often in women. If your brain already has a sufficient supply of dopamine, you won't feel any different after eating chicken or beef. Because of estrogen, most women are sensitive to the effects of carbohydrate on serotonin, and not the effects of protein on dopamine.

Nonetheless, there may be occasions when the protein cravings override the carbohydrate cravings. Whether it's because of dwindling dopamine levels or manufacturing muscle mass, your body is trying to send you a food message. Listen to it!

"Why do I sometimes have an overwhelming craving for red meat? Not fish, not chicken breast, not legumes—only a rare, juicy steak?" You may be craving the protein, but most likely, your body is probably craving iron too. Red meat has the most available form of iron for your body. If you crave red

•

Food	Do You Like It? (like, dislike, neutral)	Do You Crave It? (never, sometimes, often)	Do You Eat It? (never, sometimes, often)	How Do You Feel After Eating?
beef	_____	_____	_____	_____
chicken breast	_____	_____	_____	_____
chicken leg	_____	_____	_____	_____
turkey	_____	_____	_____	_____
pork	_____	_____	_____	_____
lamb	_____	_____	_____	_____
veal	_____	_____	_____	_____
venison	_____	_____	_____	_____
duck	_____	_____	_____	_____
salmon	_____	_____	_____	_____
trout	_____	_____	_____	_____
sole	_____	_____	_____	_____
halibut	_____	_____	_____	_____
cod	_____	_____	_____	_____
shrimp	_____	_____	_____	_____
scallops	_____	_____	_____	_____
lobster	_____	_____	_____	_____
clams	_____	_____	_____	_____
oysters	_____	_____	_____	_____
crab	_____	_____	_____	_____
tofu	_____	_____	_____	_____
legumes	_____	_____	_____	_____
milk	_____	_____	_____	_____
cottage cheese	_____	_____	_____	_____
yogurt	_____	_____	_____	_____
cheese	_____	_____	_____	_____

●

meat, and only red meat, no other color—it's the iron your body wants. So give your body iron!

Which protein foods are your female pleasure foods?

All women need some protein daily and experience occasional protein cravings. To help you identify your female protein pleasure foods, rate yet another list with your preferences, how often you crave them, how often you eat them, and how the foods make you feel.

How often do you crave high-protein foods that you dislike?

How often do you crave high-protein foods that you feel neutral about?

How often do you crave high-protein foods that you like and that make you feel good? **These are your female pleasure foods.** Go back to the list and circle all your high protein female pleasure foods.

How often do you eat foods that you like, crave, and make you feel good?

There is one last female food craving category to discuss that I'm sure you've been wondering about—salt.

SALT: YOUR PREMENSTRUAL PAL

"I understand my cravings and preferences for starch, sugar, fat, chocolate, and even protein sometimes—but what about salt! You haven't even discussed it yet. The day before I start my period, I'll buy pretzels just so I can pick the salt off. I've even put salt on my palm and licked it off. Sometimes, I think I crave salt even more than I crave chocolate."

Salt cravings are almost as common premenstrually as chocolate cravings. I haven't discussed salt yet because it has not been found to affect a woman's moods. The food-mood connection is such a new area of research that who knows

•

what will be discovered in the future. But, as with everything else, there is a biological explanation to help you understand, accept, and work with your salt cravings.

The basis of the explanation is the same for all female food cravings: estrogen. In the case of salt, however, it's not the effects of estrogen on brain chemicals, but its effects on water retention. Water retention goes by many names: "water weight," "holding water," "the Hoover Dam," "bloated." Whatever you may call it, it's real and most likely to occur in the hands, feet, ankles, face, and abdomen.

Whenever you are retaining water because of estrogen— premenstrually, with oral contraceptives, with hormone replacement therapy, or during pregnancy—your body wants to make sure it maintains a healthy balance of minerals that are dissolved in your body fluids. These minerals are called electrolytes and include a number of minerals, but salt, which contains sodium and chloride, is the most important. If you gain a couple of pounds of water weight, you will crave some salt to go along with it.

I once had a client who gained exactly twelve pounds every month. At first, it seemed impossible, but sure enough, for three consecutive months it was twelve pounds. Many of us may have different sizes of clothing in the closet depending on which side of the yo-yo diet cycle we are on. She had two sets of clothing depending on whether she was in the first or the last two weeks of her menstrual cycle.

Gaining twelve pounds of water weight is an extreme case (the average is two to four pounds), but the more fluids you retain, the more salt you will crave to balance the electrolytes. And then, if you eat too much salt, you'll retain even more fluid to balance the concentration of excessive electrolytes.

•

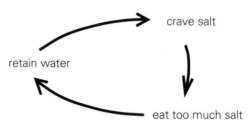

If you have a yearning for salt, give your body the small amount that it needs but not too much. How much is too much? That's a tough question to answer because it depends on how much water you retain, whether or not you have high blood pressure, and how much salt is in the food you are craving. I do not recommend adding up the milligrams of salt you eat; it's tedious and time consuming, and we all differ in the amounts we need. Instead, listen to your body and eat a very small amount of whatever it is. Think about the ramifications of eating too much salt, gaining more water weight, then craving more salt, etc.

Eating a moderate amount of salt will prevent further weight gain, but what can you do to lose those few extra pounds premenstrually or with estrogen replacement?

Here are some suggestions:

1. Exercise! The increase in body temperature and sweating allows for excess water to be removed through the skin.
2. Drinks lots of water. Water acts like a natural diuretic by stimulating more frequent urination.
3. Consume other natural diuretics: cucumbers, grapefruit, watermelon, or squeeze half a lemon in your water.

Sometimes it can be difficult to figure out exactly what you are craving: salt, fat, sugar, or starch. Take potato chips, for example. They are high in salt, but also high in fat and

•

starch. So, how can you tell which one you are craving? Do an experiment. First try salted pretzels; if they satisfy your craving, then it was the salt your body really wanted. If pretzels weren't satisfying, try unsalted potato chips. If they were satisfying, then your body was going for the fat. If neither was satisfying, it was the fat-salt combination.

Which high-salt foods are your female pleasure foods?

Here's the last list to identify your female pleasure foods. You know what to do.

Food	Do You Like It? (like, dislike, neutral)	Do You Crave It? (never, sometimes, often)	Do You Eat It? (never, sometimes, often)	How Do You Feel After Eating?
salt	_____	_____	_____	_____
salted snacks	_____	_____	_____	_____
salted crackers	_____	_____	_____	_____
canned soup	_____	_____	_____	_____
canned tomatoes	_____	_____	_____	_____
pickles	_____	_____	_____	_____
olives	_____	_____	_____	_____
cheese	_____	_____	_____	_____
cold cuts	_____	_____	_____	_____
bacon	_____	_____	_____	_____
sausage	_____	_____	_____	_____
pizza	_____	_____	_____	_____
Chinese food	_____	_____	_____	_____

How often do you crave high-salt foods that you dislike?

How often do you crave high-salt foods that you feel neutral about?

How often do you crave high-salt foods that you like and

•

that make you feel good? **These are your female pleasure foods.** Go back to the list and circle them.

How often do you eat the foods that you like, you crave, and make you feel good?

We have discussed six different categories of potential female food cravings: starch, sugar, fat, chocolate, protein, and salt. Women do crave other female pleasure foods such as vegetables for nutrients, dairy products for calcium, and water for hydration—but I'm going to save their benefits to the female body for the last chapter, on Empowerment Eating, which will address all of our special nutritional needs.

Based on your responses to the food list questionnaires:

- Which food categories include the majority of your pleasure foods?
- Are all categories of equal importance?
- Does one category rise above the others?

After answering these questions, go back to the lists in this chapter and choose your top 10 pleasure foods list. These are the foods that will be especially helpful when you know you biologically need something, but can't pinpoint exactly what it is. Check out your top 10 list and see if something jumps out at you.

•

Your Top 10 Female Pleasure Foods

1. _____
2. _____
3. _____
4. _____
5. _____
6. _____
7. _____
8. _____
9. _____
10. _____

Many of my clients ask me to reveal my top 10 pleasure foods list, so you may be wondering too. Not necessarily in any particular order, they are: potato chips, cheese pizza, chocolate cake, chocolate chip cookies, pasta, bagels, spinach, Swiss chard, potatoes, and soup.

STOP! ARE YOU EXPERIENCING A BIOLOGICAL FEMALE FOOD CRAVING RIGHT NOW?

If you are, and you are hungry, go satisfy that craving. It's one of your female pleasure foods.

Now that you have all the knowledge and skills to Discover Your Female Pleasure Foods, let's put this second step into practice.

•

WEEK 2: Your **ON** Action Plan

STEP 2: Discover Your Female Pleasure Foods

GOALS:
1. Identify all your pleasure foods.
2. Eat the foods you like and crave most often.
3. Continue trusting and responding to your female food cravings.

TECHNIQUES:
1. Use the starch list to discover those foods that you like, you crave, and make you feel good.
2. Use the sugar list to discover those foods that you like, you crave, and make you feel good.
3. Use the fat list to discover those foods that you like, you crave, and make you feel good.
4. Use the chocolate list to discover those foods that you like, you crave, and make you feel good.
5. Use the protein list to discover those foods that you like, you crave, and make you feel good.
6. Use the salt list to discover those foods that you like, you crave, and make you feel good.
7. Devise and use your top 10 female pleasure foods list.
8. Eat sugar with starch to prevent the sugar-high/sugar-low response.
9. Use the Hunger/Fullness Rating Scale.

•

10. Use the Mood Scale.
11. Keep eating records for the next week to practice these techniques.

During this second week of the **ON** Plan, the goal is to discover all of your female pleasure foods and to begin experiencing their benefits. As with the first week, I encourage you to keep eating records to gain a greater awareness and monitor your progress.

On the following pages are a sample eating record and a blank record to use for the next week. You will continue checking in with your body every hour or so to see if it is craving anything, how hungry it is, and what mood it's in. The additional focus will be on *eating* your female pleasure foods and noticing the benefits in mood as a result of responding to your body's needs.

•

EATING RECORDS TO DISCOVER
YOUR FEMALE PLEASURE FOODS

Time	Food Craving	Hunger Level	Mood State	Did You Eat Your Pleasure Food?	Mood State After Eating
____	_____	_____	_____	_____	_____
____	_____	_____	_____	_____	_____
____	_____	_____	_____	_____	_____
____	_____	_____	_____	_____	_____
____	_____	_____	_____	_____	_____
____	_____	_____	_____	_____	_____
____	_____	_____	_____	_____	_____
____	_____	_____	_____	_____	_____
____	_____	_____	_____	_____	_____
____	_____	_____	_____	_____	_____
____	_____	_____	_____	_____	_____
____	_____	_____	_____	_____	_____
____	_____	_____	_____	_____	_____
____	_____	_____	_____	_____	_____
____	_____	_____	_____	_____	_____
____	_____	_____	_____	_____	_____
____	_____	_____	_____	_____	_____
____	_____	_____	_____	_____	_____
____	_____	_____	_____	_____	_____
____	_____	_____	_____	_____	_____
____	_____	_____	_____	_____	_____
____	_____	_____	_____	_____	_____
____	_____	_____	_____	_____	_____

•

EATING RECORDS TO DISCOVER
YOUR FEMALE PLEASURE FOODS

Time	Food Craving	Hunger Level	Mood State	Did You Eat Your Pleasure Food?	Mood State After Eating
____	_____	_____	_____	_____	_____
____	_____	_____	_____	_____	_____
____	_____	_____	_____	_____	_____
____	_____	_____	_____	_____	_____
____	_____	_____	_____	_____	_____
____	_____	_____	_____	_____	_____
____	_____	_____	_____	_____	_____
____	_____	_____	_____	_____	_____
____	_____	_____	_____	_____	_____
____	_____	_____	_____	_____	_____
____	_____	_____	_____	_____	_____
____	_____	_____	_____	_____	_____
____	_____	_____	_____	_____	_____
____	_____	_____	_____	_____	_____
____	_____	_____	_____	_____	_____
____	_____	_____	_____	_____	_____
____	_____	_____	_____	_____	_____
____	_____	_____	_____	_____	_____
____	_____	_____	_____	_____	_____
____	_____	_____	_____	_____	_____
____	_____	_____	_____	_____	_____
____	_____	_____	_____	_____	_____

•

Six

OF COURSE, WE ALL KNOW the mechanics of eating: open package, prepare food, bring fork to mouth, and insert food. But I'm not talking about the mechanics of eating, I'm talking about the process of eating. What goes on in your eyes, mouth, nose, stomach, and brain—and how the responses from each of these brings feelings of satisfaction to the eating experience.

In Step 2, you identified the foods most likely to give your body and brain optimal pleasure. The next step of the **ON** Plan is to learn how to eat those foods to turn *on* your food satisfaction, energy level, and positive moods most effectively.

You may have thought that as long as you eat your female pleasure foods, you'll feel satisfied. Maybe, maybe not. It all depends on *how* you eat those pleasure foods and the six stages of eating satisfaction.

•

The Six Stages of Satisfaction

1. visual satisfaction
2. taste bud satisfaction
3. olfactory (nose) satisfaction
4. stomach satisfaction
5. bloodstream satisfaction
6. brain satisfaction

There is a true science to feeling satisfied with food, a science that begins with the visual pleasure of food before you even start eating. If the food is pleasing to the eye, it will be pleasing to the brain. Sometimes setting a formal table with flowers and candlelight can add to the satisfaction you will receive from eating. Does the presentation of the food look appetizing? Are there various colors, textures, and forms? Or, does the plate look like a 1920s black-and-white movie, void of stimulating colors?

The more satisfied you are with the visual quality of the food as well as each of the other stages of satisfaction, the less you'll need to eat, and the better you'll feel. Your brain is the receiving center for all six stages, and the goal is to experience maximum satisfaction every step of the way. Here are some secrets to guarantee high-level satisfaction.

THE SECRETS OF TASTE BUD SATISFACTION

What goes on in your mouth while you are eating is as important as what goes on in your body and brain after you eat. Your taste buds are in direct communication with your brain to determine the palatability of the food and to give your brain a preview of what's to come. Your brain *always* wants to know what's going on.

•

I'm sure that most of you have heard that there are four different sets of taste buds on your tongue: sweet, sour, salty, and bitter. But did you know that you have thousands of taste detectors, called chemoreceptors, on your taste buds? When you eat, these chemoreceptors are stimulated and send pleasure signals to your brain.

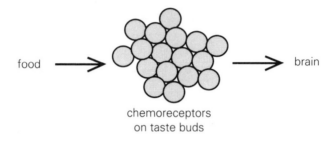

food → chemoreceptors on taste buds → brain

The greater the number of chemoreceptors stimulated, the greater the food satisfaction. The goal is to stimulate as many of the chemoreceptors as you possibly can. How? **Chew, savor, and let the food linger.**

If you eat quickly and barely chew your food, there is minimal stimulation of the chemoreceptors and thus minimal satisfaction. Pardon the comparison, but if you eat like a snake and practically swallow your food whole without chewing, those chemoreceptors didn't have the time or the means to be stimulated. The bite was too big and it went by too quickly. They vaguely remember something passing by, but couldn't tell what it was. Your brain has no idea what's going on, and you don't feel satisfied.

"I'd have to say that I eat like a snake, but don't snakes eat only once a week? I may share a snake's chewing habits, but definitely not its eating habits." Then Nadine asked, "Since we are on animal comparisons, what animal should I model my chewing after?"

•

How about . . . a cow? Disregarding the physical image, if you eat like a cow (not the grass, but the way they chew, and chew, and chew the grass), your chemoreceptors are stimulated, happy, busy shooting off one message after another to your brain. Your brain is already starting to feel satisfied from the happiness of the taste buds even before you've swallowed the food.

Chewing has another benefit. It enhances the release of aromas, allows you to fully capture the smell of food, and stimulates the olfactory nerves in your brain. Your sense of smell accounts for almost 50 percent of the initial satisfaction from eating; therefore, your nose and taste buds are partners in providing satisfaction. This collaboration explains the blandness of food when you have a cold. If you barely chew your food, your taste buds and your nose are both in the dark—and your brain is thinking about taking a nap.

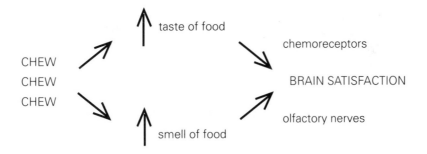

"Are you going to tell me to chew each bite twenty-five times to maximize satisfaction? I've tried it, I lose count, and it doesn't work." Don't worry, unlike some books or programs, I am not going to recommend that you count your chews or chew a certain number of times per bite. I will, however, recommend that you fully understand the importance of taste bud satisfaction and focus on *the first three bites.*

Why the first three bites? Because research has shown

•

that the first three bites are the most important in satisfying your taste buds, chemoreceptors, nose, and brain. The first bite emits the strongest stimulation, the second bite a little less, and the third even less. By the time you've taken your fourth or fifth bite, your taste buds are starting to get bored, and they really don't care what's going on anymore. Their job is done.

When I discuss the secrets of taste bud satisfaction, I always think of my sister, Lori. Ever since I can remember, she has cut her food up into minuscule pieces and fully enjoyed the eating experience. By the time she had chewed and swallowed the first three bites, most of the other family members had finished eating. Food satisfaction is more important to her than to anyone else I know, including myself. She has always eaten what she wanted, satisfied her food cravings, and maintained a healthy weight. With three boys now (two still in diapers), she doesn't have the luxury of taking a half hour or so to enjoy her meal. To adjust to her lifestyle, she has taken her sister's advice and used the first-three-bite approach to satisfaction.

Our taste buds are designed not only to provide pleasure and satisfaction but also to protect us. Our sweet taste buds are located on the tip of our tongue, giving sugar detection a lead on other flavors. There is a purpose for this. Sugar is concentrated in calories, and during times of famine and food deprivation, our sweet preference ensured survival. We like the taste of sugar because we evolved that way. The very young and the very old have an even greater affinity for sweets because it would be harder for them to forage for food in times of scarcity, and their desire for sweet foods provided the most calories.

Our other taste buds also have protective purposes:

•

- Salty: We would die without salt. Our salt taste buds encouraged a liking for salty foods for the purpose of survival. Before the salt shaker or processed foods, we relied on our taste buds to detect even small amounts of salt in roots, berries, and other plants.
- Bitter: When we were scavenging for food, we would try just about any living plant. To prevent us from eating the poisonous plants, the bitter taste buds alerted us to toxic chemicals.
- Sour: Our bodies need a certain acid/base balance, and the sour taste buds prevented us from eating too many acidic foods.

You may be wondering if there are gender differences in taste buds and chemoreceptors. As you suspected, women's sweet taste buds do a better job at communicating with the brain. In the case of famine and the need for survival, our sweet taste buds evolved to make the higher-calorie sugar foods taste better to us. Our bitter taste buds are also more evolved to detect toxic substances and prevent poisoning. This discriminating ability explains the common food aversions to coffee, alcohol, and spicy foods during the first trimester of pregnancy.

To summarize the secrets of taste bud satisfaction:

1. Satisfy your female food cravings with pleasure foods.
2. Chew, Chew, Chew.
3. Take the time to smell the food.
4. Eat slowly, savor each bite, and let the food linger.
5. Focus on the first three bites.

"Are you telling me that I only need to chew, smell, and savor the first three bites of chocolate, ice cream, or anything

•

else to experience maximum satisfaction?" Technically, yes—
at least for the first stage of satisfaction. But there are other
stages of satisfaction to tell you about.

THE SECRETS OF STOMACH SATISFACTION

From the taste buds, we move on to the stomach. You've
taken a small bite of food, you've chewed it thoroughly,
you've stimulated the chemoreceptors and the olfactory
nerves in your brain, and thus you've already achieved a certain level of satisfaction.

Now the food is traveling down your esophagus and is
about to pass into the stomach. Because the taste buds have
informed your brain that something pleasurable is on its way,
your brain has already alerted the stomach to the pending arrival of food; some digestive enzymes have been secreted, and
they are lying in waiting for the food. By the time the first
three bites have entered your stomach, it is already starting to
feel content.

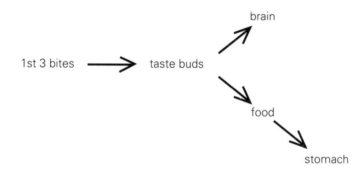

"How can just a few bites of food excite my stomach? I
usually stuff one hundred-plus bites of food in there. Why
don't I automatically stop at three bites?"

Well, you may not have known, and, therefore, not experienced the first stage of taste bud satisfaction. Your stomach
wasn't informed and wasn't ready. Or, you may have been

•

overeating for so long that you aren't aware of what's going on in your stomach and how small your stomach really is.

Hold up a clenched fist. That's the approximate size of your stomach. You can see why you need only a few bites for your stomach to start feeling satisfied.

"If my stomach is the size of my fist, how on earth have I ever been able to fit a sixteen-inch pepperoni pizza in there? Or my Thanksgiving dinner? Or last Saturday night's dinner at my favorite Italian restaurant?" Katie was amazed by the fist comparison. Probably to prevent your stomach from erupting—which would cause immediate death—its stretching capability makes it possible to devour unbelievably huge quantities at times. A morbid explanation—but there is one documented death of a bulimic who consumed 50,000 calories at one meal.

Your stomach can expand to about five times its original size, but it doesn't necessarily want to expand. Like the receptors on your taste buds, receptors are also on the wall of your stomach. From the first bite to the time when the fist-sized stomach is filled, those receptors are shooting off signals to the brain, and a chemical is released from your stomach and intestine called cholecystokinin (we'll call it CCK).

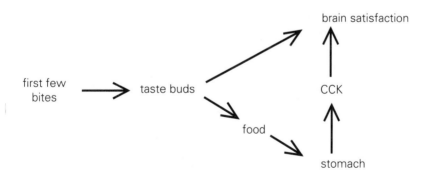

CCK is a satiety chemical that tells your brain eating really did happen, and you weren't just daydreaming about a

•

pizza. It's a feedback mechanism that makes you feel satisfied and reminds you to stop eating.

"Is it possible that I was born without this CCK? I don't think I have a feedback mechanism to make me stop eating. Where can I go to get an injection?" Sally isn't the first person to ask me these questions. Although a handful of bulimics have been found to be deficient in CCK, we all have it; we just don't listen to it. Or we eat so quickly that we've gone beyond the point of satisfaction without realizing it until later.

This need to respond to our feedback mechanism is why some weight control experts have recommended taking twenty minutes to eat every meal. Although there is no hard scientific data to support the twenty-minute recommendation, it is true that the more slowly you eat, the more likely you'll be aware of the CCK feedback mechanism and stop eating when you feel comfortably satisfied.

Slow down your eating as much as you can, and:

1. Use your fist to determine a satisfying amount of food for your stomach.
2. Allow the CCK to accurately inform your brain of stomach satisfaction.
3. Once again, focus on the first 3 bites.

The final stage of satisfaction is called the postabsorptive effect of food—what happens after the food has been absorbed into your bloodstream and passes through the blood-brain barrier. These are the effects of food on your blood glucose levels and your brain chemicals. We've already discussed these postabsorptive effects of food in a great deal of depth, but let's review it so that you have the entire picture.

You're hungry and have a craving for a specific pleasure food, you focus on the first three bites, and your taste buds and nose send satisfaction signals to your brain. Then you swallow the food, and your stomach sends its satisfaction sig-

•

nals to your brain. The food is then absorbed into your bloodstream, passes through the blood-brain barrier, and your brain is satisfied with the supply of energy and brain chemicals. Throughout this process, your brain is intimately involved in every stage of food satisfaction.

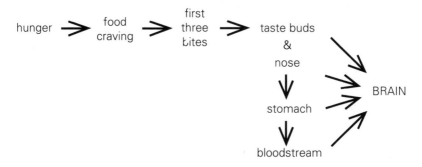

With your new knowledge of the secrets of satisfaction, you can now experience the pleasure every step of the way. When you do, you'll eat *less* and enjoy the food *more*. What you crave is what will be most satisfying to you. If you search for substitutes to your cravings, however, no matter how much you try to employ these secrets of satisfaction, you'll come up short.

SUBSTITUTES DON'T SATISFY

In an attempt to satisfy cravings without calories, women are consuming more artificial sweeteners and fake fats each year. Fake foods do not satisfy cravings for most people because they don't have the same effects in the bloodstream and brain that real food does.

If you have a hankering for something sweet, but are fearful of calories and weight gain, you may go for diet Jell-O instead. The artificial sweetener tastes like sugar and your stimulated taste buds send messages to your brain. When the diet Jell-O enters your stomach, the receptors acknowledge

•

that something has entered and CCK is released to your brain. So you do get the initial stages of satisfaction. But the satisfaction stops here. **You can fool your taste buds, but not your brain.**

The brain is not getting what it needs to function from the fake sugar. Once it is absorbed into your bloodstream, your blood sugar does not increase because it wasn't broken down to glucose molecules. The artificial sweetener does enter into your brain cells, but does not provide the building blocks for serotonin. Your brain is expecting a load of sugar because the taste buds detected sweetness and sent a message to your brain, but when instead the fake sugar knocks on the door, your brain is not just unsatisfied—it's dissatisfied. So, it may start urging you to eat real, nature-made sugar.

This explains the paradox of our sugar consumption over the last fifty years: As our intake of artificial sweeteners has increased, so, too, has our intake of sugar. For most people, artificial sweeteners have not been an effective substitute for sugar in our diets; they have not helped us to lose weight or reduce our sugar intake, and they may be responsible for increasing our sugar intake. Using artificial sweeteners has similar effects to those brought on by deprivation and abstinence. You don't feel satisfied, the craving intensifies, you end up eating the sugar anyway—and more of it.

Fake fats rob you of food satisfaction even more than fake sugars. Most people have reported that fat substitutes are not palatable and, therefore, do not produce the initial taste bud satisfaction. Then, when they are absorbed, they also don't produce brain satisfaction. Fake fats, thus, deprive you of most stages of satisfaction.

So, fake foods are not satisfying substitutes, but even real food substitutes may not provide the level of satisfaction you are looking for. If you try to satisfy an ice cream craving with nonfat cottage cheese, will you achieve the same satisfaction?

•

Or a craving for caramel with carrot sticks? You'll end up "eating around the craving" for a while without deriving satisfaction, then consume the ice cream or caramel anyway. **Satisfy the *real* craving by slowly eating a small amount.**

What about a substitute for chocolate? If you search the cupboards and refrigerator for a substitute for chocolate, you'll come up empty-handed. There is no substitute for chocolate. Carob is often suggested as a chocolate substitute because it has the same color and consistency, but it is made from a Mediterranean evergreen tree, not the cocoa plant. It has no phenylethylamine, no theobromine—and no satisfaction.

White chocolate doesn't work either for the same reasons—no mood-altering phenylethylamine and theobromine. It is a confection made with sugar and fat, so it will satisfy a sugar and/or a fat craving, but not a chocolate craving.

Based on consumer demand, many food companies, bakeries, and cookbooks are now offering lower fat chocolate products. Less fat does not have to mean less satisfaction, as long as they pleasure your palate and brain.

Don't search for unsatisfying substitutes, eat exactly what you want, and focus on the secrets of satisfaction. To achieve the highest level of satisfaction, there are two more concepts to share that enhance the postabsorptive benefits of food and fully satisfy the brain.

GAINING THE COMPETITIVE FOOD-MOOD EDGE

Some food-mood competition is going on that you need to know about. What you eat with your mood-enhancing female pleasure foods can interfere with the expected benefit. You already know that:

•

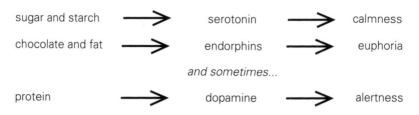

| sugar and starch | → | serotonin | → | calmness |
| chocolate and fat | → | endorphins | → | euphoria |

and sometimes...

| protein | → | dopamine | → | alertness |

But, if you are craving carbohydrates *and* eat protein with them, you'll be waiting forever for the calmness to take effect. It's almost like a football game—the carbohydrate team vs. the protein team—and the protein team wins. Protein will block the release of serotonin in your brain.

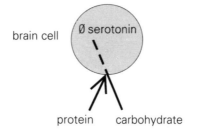

When you crave carbohydrates, you need the serotonin release, but if meat, fish, poultry, or milk products are eaten with the serotonin-releasing carbohydrates, you won't feel calm, stable, and content. This is why the traditional balanced meal approach doesn't balance a woman's mind and moods.

Let's digest the typical meal of steak, potato, vegetable, bread, and salad. The steak introduces too much competition for the potato and bread to handle (but the vegetable and salad produce no problem at all!).

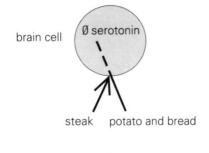

•

The typical lunch repeats the no-win situation for serotonin. Lunch is usually a sandwich with two slices of bread, three ounces of meat, lettuce, tomato, mustard, and mayonnaise. You may think the bread will calm you and rejuvenate your energy—but the turkey or ham or roast beef will negate the calming effects of the bread. The same holds true for the peanut butter you put on the English muffin, the cheese you put on the cracker, and the milk you drink with the pretzels.

If you crave carbohydrates for the calming effects of serotonin, watch out for eating protein along with it. This doesn't hold true the other way around. If you are craving protein for dopamine or muscle needs, carbohydrates do not cause any threat at all. Protein always has the competitive edge.

There are two food-mood competition rules:

Rule #1: When you are craving carbohydrates, beware of protein.

Rule #2: When you are craving carbohydrates or protein, beware of too much fat.

Too much fat can also interfere with the carbohydrate-serotonin brain benefit, but in a different way from protein. Fat interferes by causing some competition in the stomach instead of in the brain. Fat takes a long, long time to digest and slows down the absorption of glucose. The glucose is trying to enter the bloodstream but is being held captive by the undigested fat.

fat   takes 5 hours to digest
starch takes 2 hours to digest
sugar   takes ¼ hour to digest

If you put just a small amount of butter on your English muffin, the carbohydrates will still be normally digested, and

•

your brain will be satisfied. But, if you soak your English muffin with butter or put a ¼-inch slab of cream cheese on your bagel, digestion will take too long, and your brain will get impatient as it is waiting for the glucose and serotonin.

I'm not necessarily recommending that you put butter on your English muffin, but a small amount will not cause any food-mood competition. Better yet, how about trying jam on the English muffin? The jam would complement (not compete with) the serotonin release.

Selectively choose *what* you eat with your craved carbohydrate foods to gain the competitive food-mood edge—and be conscious of *how much* you're eating.

OVEREATING OVERLOADS THE BRAIN

Whether it's a combination of foods or a single food, a meal or a snack, I think it's time to do a reality check by discussing amounts in more detail. Some clients pray that I will tell them, "You need a pound of chocolate, a loaf of bread, and a quart of ice cream." Sorry—if the craving is truly biological, a very small amount is all it takes to pleasure your mouth, stomach, and brain. Here are some examples:

> 1 piece of bread
> 1 medium fruit
> ½ cup of fruit juice
> ½ ounce of chocolate
> ¼ cup of ice cream
> 5 gumdrops

"Five gumdrops—you've got to be joking. Fifty maybe, five never. Wouldn't eating fifty gumdrops give me ten times the benefit of five? And what if I ate five ounces of chocolate, wouldn't it give me ten times the benefit of half an ounce?"

•

It doesn't work that way. A small amount is all that it takes to maximize the benefits from food, and eating more does not provide more benefit. To the contrary, eating more diminishes the benefit. It's called the "overload effect."

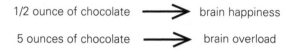

Your brain put in a request for assistance, and you sent in the armed forces. Your brain is bombarded, not to mention you have a stomachache and have activated your fat cells.

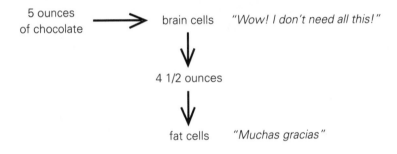

"I understand that eating too much chocolate or too much of anything will activate my fat cells, but what about all those calories burned carrying around those five ounces, hiding it all around the house, trying to find where you hid it, and unwrapping each piece individually?" Valerie and I figured it out: 750 calories in the chocolate versus 50 calories laboring the chocolate.

Another reason why overeating results in brain shock is that your brain is dependent on a steady supply of blood. When you overeat, your blood supply is directed to the stomach for the lengthy digestive process, leaving your brain deprived of oxygen, nutrients, and glucose. For lack of any other alternative, your brain waves start to slow down and you may enter stage one of sleep.

•

Many clients want me to go through hundreds of foods and specifically quantify how much they need to eat to satisfy a biological food craving. Maryann wanted to know, "Exactly how many M&M's, caramel candies, and strands of licorice?" She would eat exactly that amount, no more and no less. Please don't take the amounts too literally. When I say four jelly beans, it doesn't mean exactly four, never three and never five. The point I'm repeatedly trying to make is that self-indulgence is achieved with a very small amount and overeating overloads the brain.

> **STOP! ARE YOU EXPERIENCING A BIOLOGICAL FEMALE FOOD CRAVING RIGHT NOW?**

If you are, go satisfy that craving with a small amount, beware of food-mood competition, and savor the first three bites.

Now that you have all the knowledge and skills to Eat for Maximum Satisfaction, let's put this step into practice.

•

WEEK 3: Your **ON** Action Plan

STEP 3: Learn How to Eat for Maximum Satisfaction

GOALS:
1. Master the secrets of taste bud satisfaction.
2. Experience stomach satisfaction.
3. Gain the competitive food-mood edge.
4. Practice self-indulgence without overindulgence.

TECHNIQUES:
1. Make your meal visually pleasing.
2. Chew thoroughly.
3. Eat like a cow, not like a snake.
4. Focus on the first three bites.
5. Eat slowly and let the food linger.
6. Take the time to smell the food.
7. Use the first comparison.
8. Don't search for unsatisfying substitutes.
9. Beware of protein competition.
10. Beware of fat competition.
11. Use the Hunger/Fullness Rating Scale to prevent overeating.
12. Use the Mood List.
13. Use the Satisfaction Scale.
14. Keep eating records for the next week to practice these techniques.

You are now beginning the third week of the **ON** Plan. This week, I still want you to continue assessing your hunger, mood, and discovering your pleasure foods—but I also want you to focus on achieving maximum satisfaction from the

•

taste buds, nose, stomach, and brain. Keep in mind that satisfaction is also influenced by food-mood competition and the amounts you are eating. To help you achieve satisfaction, use this satisfaction scale:

> 5—maximum satisfaction
> 4—moderate satisfaction
> 3—neutral
> 2—moderate dissatisfaction
> 1—complete dissatisfaction

Remember: the more satisfied you are with the eating experience, the less you will need to eat.

On the following pages is a sample eating record along with a blank record to use for the next week. We will continue to build on all your skills, so in addition to rating hunger and mood (before and after you eat), you will also assess your level of fullness, your level of satisfaction, and whether there was any food-mood competition. Use the above satisfaction scale, as well as the Hunger/Fullness Rating Scale from Chapter 4 to rate your fullness level and prevent overloading your brain and activating your fat cells. Whenever you are above level 5 (perfectly comfortable)—you are overeating!

•

EATING RECORDS FOR MAXIMUM SATISFACTION

Time	Food Craving	Hunger Level	Mood State	Any Food-Mood Compe-tition?	Fullness Level	Mood State	Satis-faction
——	——	——	——	——	——	——	——
——	——	——	——	——	——	——	——
——	——	——	——	——	——	——	——
——	——	——	——	——	——	——	——
——	——	——	——	——	——	——	——
——	——	——	——	——	——	——	——
——	——	——	——	——	——	——	——
——	——	——	——	——	——	——	——
——	——	——	——	——	——	——	——
——	——	——	——	——	——	——	——
——	——	——	——	——	——	——	——
——	——	——	——	——	——	——	——
——	——	——	——	——	——	——	——
——	——	——	——	——	——	——	——
——	——	——	——	——	——	——	——
——	——	——	——	——	——	——	——
——	——	——	——	——	——	——	——
——	——	——	——	——	——	——	——
——	——	——	——	——	——	——	——
——	——	——	——	——	——	——	——
——	——	——	——	——	——	——	——
——	——	——	——	——	——	——	——
——	——	——	——	——	——	——	——
——	——	——	——	——	——	——	——
——	——	——	——	——	——	——	——

•

EATING RECORDS FOR MAXIMUM SATISFACTION

Time	Food Craving	Hunger Level	Mood State	Any Food-Mood Compe- tition?	Fullness Level	Mood State	Satis- faction
___	___	___	___	___	___	___	___
___	___	___	___	___	___	___	___
___	___	___	___	___	___	___	___
___	___	___	___	___	___	___	___
___	___	___	___	___	___	___	___
___	___	___	___	___	___	___	___
___	___	___	___	___	___	___	___
___	___	___	___	___	___	___	___
___	___	___	___	___	___	___	___
___	___	___	___	___	___	___	___
___	___	___	___	___	___	___	___
___	___	___	___	___	___	___	___
___	___	___	___	___	___	___	___
___	___	___	___	___	___	___	___
___	___	___	___	___	___	___	___
___	___	___	___	___	___	___	___
___	___	___	___	___	___	___	___
___	___	___	___	___	___	___	___
___	___	___	___	___	___	___	___
___	___	___	___	___	___	___	___
___	___	___	___	___	___	___	___
___	___	___	___	___	___	___	___
___	___	___	___	___	___	___	___

•

Seven

STEP 4:

DISTRIBUTE YOUR FOOD TO

MAXIMIZE MOOD

J ANET, THE ONLY FEMALE PARTNER in a prestigious law firm, shared with me what had happened at a recent fiscal planning meeting. "We had been focused on intense discussions for three straight hours, when all of a sudden, I felt my energy dwindling, my mind wandering, and my stomach growling. I glanced at my watch and sure enough, just as I suspected, it was 3:45 P.M. I stood up and announced, "Excuse me, gentlemen, my brain needs some chocolate. It's time for my afternoon stamina snack." It was actually entertaining to watch their confused faces as I left the room, and even more entertaining to see their surprised expressions when I returned rejuvenated and ready to go for the next three hours."

Janet knew the benefit of responding to her body's needs throughout the day, and made it a priority at work and at home. She also knew that the afternoon snack was vital to keep her efficient female brain working at top capacity. The

•

afternoon snack, however, is not the only important "meal time" for women. There are other specific hours of the day when our brains have open lines of communication to our food cravings.

I suspect that you've already come to a few awarenesses about the timing of eating and how it influences your food cravings and mood states. Most women report that their strongest and most beneficial food cravings occur in the afternoon. This is not coincidental. A woman's brain chemicals are most likely to be influenced in the midday hours, and what you eat midday will greatly influence how you feel and what you crave in the late afternoon. Then, what you eat in the late afternoon will greatly influence how you feel and what you crave in the evening. If you don't respond to your food cravings during the day, they will escalate at night.

When it comes to women, food cravings, and well-being —timing is everything. We've all used the phrase "I was at the right place at the right time" in reference to getting a job or meeting a significant other. Because timing is everything with regard to your female food needs, a similar phrase can be used with your food-mood connection: "I must have eaten the right foods at the right time because I feel revitalized."

With the first three steps of the **ON** Plan, you have discovered your pleasure foods in the starch, sugar, fat, chocolate, protein, and salt categories. You also have learned how to eat those foods to achieve maximum benefit and satisfaction. The next step of the **ON** Plan is to learn *when* to eat and how to distribute your female pleasure foods most effectively to:

- stabilize your blood sugar
- enhance your brain chemicals
- benefit your female body and brain

•

FIVE SMALL MEALS FOR BIG BENEFITS

By making the **ON** Plan a part of her life, Denise found that her body had automatically gravitated toward smaller, more frequent meals throughout the day. As she expressed it, "Of course women should be eating five times a day. If we satisfy our cravings when we are hungry with a small amount, we should expect to receive food messages every few hours." Denise was right on target, and if you haven't experienced more frequent food messages yet, expect to be hungry four or five times a day—and by responding to that hunger, expect great improvements in your performance.

Great things come in small packages. Five small meals a day will give you big benefits. How big? Well, by distributing your food intake into five small, evenly dispersed meals throughout the day you will:

1. keep your brain energized with a constant supply of sugar
2. prevent negative mood changes caused by low blood sugar
3. temper sugar cravings caused by low blood sugar
4. better manage the stress in your life
5. reduce PMS and menopausal tension
6. prevent the starvation response elicited by skipping meals
7. lose weight because you'll never be overeating and never be putting your body in the storage mode
8. experience more energy in all that you do—including your exercise program.

You have nothing to lose (except excess weight, mood swings, and fatigue), and everything to gain by eating five small meals throughout the day. And all of these big benefits are achieved through one method—keeping your blood-sugar levels stable throughout the day.

•

Because of female hormones, a woman's body and brain are sensitive to drops in blood sugar levels. This sensitivity doesn't necessarily mean that you are hypoglycemic (although a few of you may be) and have blood sugar levels critically below normal levels; it means that even minor fluctuations in blood sugar can affect your brain energy. Why? Because estrogen increases insulin sensitivity and makes insulin do a better job at transporting the glucose molecules out of the blood and into our cells. After a meal or a snack, a woman's blood sugar drops more quickly than a man's, and within a couple of hours, the brain's fuel supply is running on empty and energy is running low.

This accelerated drop in blood sugar explains why skipping meals is detrimental to our mental and physical performance. If you skip a meal and eat two meals a day, your blood sugar levels are dropping below normal levels between those two meals, and many hours pass before your brain gets the energy it needs. This dip in blood sugar is not acceptable to the female brain, and it protests with headaches, irritability, and fatigue. The brain thinks it's in a state of emergency, and demands, "Give me sugar right this very minute."

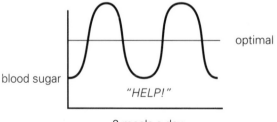

2 meals a day

If you eat the recommended three balanced meals a day, your average blood sugar levels are maintained a bit higher but still drop more than your brain would like. Your brain cannot function optimally and asks for assistance with carbohydrate cravings.

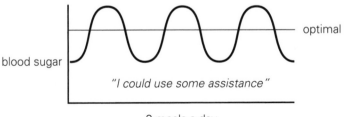

3 meals a day

No doubt, you know where I'm headed with this. If you eat five small meals a day, your blood sugar never has a chance to dip much below normal; your brain is supplied with maximal energy throughout the day, and it doesn't need to cry out with sugar cravings. In fact, it's now equipped to lend you a helping hand with brain power, creative thinking, and stable moods.

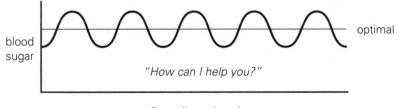

5 small meals a day

You'll notice the brain benefits of stable blood sugar levels every day, but you'll experience even more benefits during PMS, pregnancy, the menopausal transition, and when you are under stress. During these times (which for most of us is just about every day), your brain becomes even more sensitive to changes in blood sugar levels. When you let more than

•

four hours pass between meals, tension, depression, and fatigue intensify. By eating five small meals a day, you'll notice more stable moods even at some of the most unstable times.

How many meals do you eat a day?

Women on average eat only 2½ meals a day—half of what the female body needs to function at optimal levels. If you eat only two or three meals a day, you are asking your brain to work under less than optimal conditions. Would you enjoy skiing in less than optimal conditions? If you try to ski in poor conditions, you don't ski as well because you constantly have to avoid obstacles and be cautious of injury. The same constraints are true for poor brain conditions. When your brain doesn't have a sufficient sugar supply, you don't function as well, you have obstacles such as headaches and mood swings to deal with, and you are more prone to accidents because your reaction time slows.

Ask not what your brain can do for you, but what you can do for your brain.

You can give your brain five small meals a day (or at minimum four!) and the most optimal conditions for functioning. Some women are reluctant to follow this advice because of two concerns: too much food and not enough time.

"If I eat five times a day, I'll gain five pounds in a week, and expand five inches in the hips within a year." There's that number-one fear again—weight gain. If you eat five big meals a day, that fear is warranted, but I'm not talking about five big meals; I'm talking about five small meals. Confront that fear head on with the knowledge that five small meals a day will make you a smaller person. If you eat a small amount of what you crave when you are hungry, you will lose weight, not gain it. Actually, one of the most effective strategies for weight loss is to take the food you eat in two or three larger meals and divide it up into four or five smaller meals. Let me explain.

•

Women are born with the genetic programming to store fat quickly and efficiently. When we eat more calories than our bodies need to function, we quickly convert those calories (no matter where they are coming from, apples or apple pie) to fat and store them in the fat cells of our buttocks, hips, and thighs. Even if we eat just one meal a day, overeating at that meal will lead to larger fat cells and weight gain. I realize that with one meal a day you are fasting for twenty-four hours and may think that you'll simply take out what you put in, but it doesn't work that way. The stored fat stays put, and your glucose stores and muscle mass come to the rescue with the needed calories.

You could be eating the same total number of calories a day, but how you distribute those calories in the number of meals a day can lead to either weight gain or weight loss. *The choice is yours.*

1 meal of 2,000 calories	$\rightarrow$	significant weight gain
2 meals of 1,000 calories each	$\rightarrow$	moderate weight gain
4 meals of 500 calories each	$\rightarrow$	significant weight loss
5 meals of 400 calories each	$\rightarrow$	even more weight loss

(Individual daily caloric needs vary. I used 2,000 calories to make the math easy.)

A meal does not have to be meat, potato, vegetable, bread, salad, and then dessert. A meal can be as small as a snack. It can be one or two of the food groups instead of all four plus dessert. It can be all of the food groups in very small amounts. Think of eating five mini-meals (or maxi-snacks, if you'd like) a day. The goal is not to eat more food, more often; it's to take the same amount of food you eat in two or three meals a day and divide it up into five mini-meals a day—and lose weight!

•

"Okay, I understand the importance of small, frequent meals for high energy, stable moods, *and* weight loss, but I simply don't have the time. I take a three-minute shower in the morning, put on my makeup on the way to work, barely have time for bathroom breaks during the day, and rush to pick up my kids from day care after work."

Make it easy on yourself and find a way that fits into your daily lifestyle. You don't have to spend hours preparing meals, but with these simple suggestions, you can be prepared by making sure food is available:

- Split your lunch in half and save half for the afternoon snack.
- Keep a bag of pretzels or box of crackers in the glove compartment of your car.
- Keep small boxes of cereal or instant soup mixes in your office.
- Invest in a small refrigerator for your office.
- If you have a microwave in your home or office, use it. There are many low-fat microwave dinners that fit the definition of a small meal.
- Locate nearby restaurants that have take-out; some may be right around the corner.
- When you do your weekly grocery shopping, have a special list of easy meals and snacks—and stock up.

Eating five small meals a day can be a priority in your life without taking time away from your other important priorities. As a matter of fact, because of the increased energy and productivity you'll have, it will feel as if there is even more time in your day to get things done.

But, of course, *what* you eat in these five small meals can also influence your energy, productivity, cravings, and moods.

•

STABILIZING THE DESTABILIZERS

From the previous chapters, you have some knowledge of what to do to stabilize blood sugar. For example, you know that sugar is a destabilizer because of the sugar-high/sugar-low response, but you also know to eat your sugar pleasure foods with a small meal to prevent that response. In addition, there are other destabilizers to tell you about:

caffeine
alcohol
artificial sweeteners

Caffeine mobilizes glucose from your muscle and liver stores and increases the glucose supply to your brain. That's why a cup of coffee wakes you up in the morning and keeps you awake during the afternoon slump. This may sound positive, but within about an hour, blood sugar levels drop and you feel tired and unproductive. You will either (a) go for another cup of coffee to keep your brain awake or (b) go for sugar to fuel your brain.

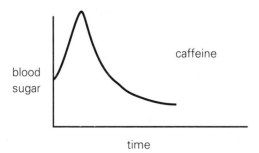

Alcohol is made from carbohydrate sources (wine from grapes, beer from barley, vodka from potatoes, etc.), so eventually it will raise blood sugar levels, but the initial effect of

•

wine, beer, or hard liquor may create a slight drop in blood sugar levels. As the liver is alerted to the presence of a drug, it boosts its metabolism to be ready to detoxify that drug, and blood sugar levels drop slightly. So, at first alcohol may stimulate your appetite, which is why it's a tradition to have a drink before dinner while dining out.

Besides caffeine and alcohol, some women may be sensitive to the effects of artificial sweeteners on blood sugar levels. In Chapter 6, we saw some of what goes on in your brain and body when you use artificial sweeteners. They may also bring about other responses. Artificial sweeteners are not real sugar sources, so they will not cause the sugar-high/sugar-low response, but they may cause a drop in blood sugar levels because of what's called the "preabsorptive insulin response." Before the saccharin or aspartame or other artificial sweetener is even absorbed in your bloodstream, a cascade of reactions can occur. Because artificial sweeteners taste like sugar, the chemoreceptors on your taste buds send "the sugar is coming, the sugar is coming" signals to your brain. Your brain is happy, and as it is anxiously awaiting the arrival of sugar, it communicates with your pancreas. "I just got a tip from the taste buds that a load of sugar is on its way; get ready with some insulin." Insulin transports sugar from your bloodstream into your cells, and by the time the artificial sweetener

•

has been absorbed (and your brain realizes that it was a false call), some insulin may have already been released from the pancreas and blood sugar levels may drop.

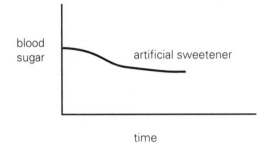

Let's do a worst-case scenario to put this all together. You overslept and don't have time for breakfast, but you always have time for a cup of coffee. You feel good for the first hour because blood sugar levels have risen, but you don't feel very good when blood sugar levels quickly drop. To help, you go for something sweet to jump-start your brain and feel good for the next half hour, but then blood sugar levels reach an all-time low. You don't have time for lunch, so you have a diet soft drink instead, another cup of coffee in the afternoon, and then a glass of wine when you get home.

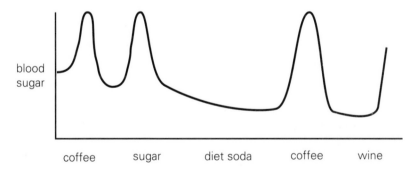

What kind of day do you think you'll have with blood sugar levels fluctuating like this? A typical day? A few short

•

bursts of hyper-energy and many hours of less than optimal functioning.

I will not recommend that you eliminate these destabilizers from your diet unless you want to. However, I will recommend that you keep two guidelines in mind. First, do not consume the destabilizers on an empty stomach; make sure they are a part of one of your five small meals. This will slow the absorption and prevent the rise and/or drop in blood sugar levels. Look at how calm and productive that typical day could have been if you had cereal with the coffee, crackers with the sugar, a sandwich with the diet soda, some pretzels with the afternoon coffee, and wine with your dinner.

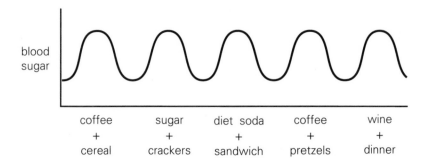

		blood sugar		
coffee	sugar	diet soda	coffee	wine
+	+	+	+	+
cereal	crackers	sandwich	pretzels	dinner

The second guideline is to keep your intakes of the destabilizers to a more moderate level. What is a moderate intake of caffeine, alcohol, and diet soft drinks? For all, the usual recommendation is 1 to 2: 1 to 2 cups of coffee, 1 to 2 alcoholic drinks, and 1 to 2 diet soft drinks.

The "two drinks or less a day" alcohol recommendation is easy to explain. One drink of alcohol is defined as 4 ounces of wine, 12 ounces of beer, or 1½ ounces of hard liquor. The coffee recommendation, however, is a bit more complicated and needs some explanation.

The "two cups or less a day" moderate recommendation

•

came out over fifteen years ago when we were percolating our coffee; two cups of percolated coffee have about 200 mg of caffeine, which is considered a moderate level. But over the last fifteen years, our brewing methods have changed dramatically, and the majority of us have replaced percolated coffee with the much stronger drip method.

1 cup of percolated coffee has 110 mg of caffeine
1 cup of drip coffee has 180 mg of caffeine

Two cups of drip coffee have 360 mg of caffeine—almost twice the moderate recommendation! Why? The finer the bean is ground, the more caffeine is extracted from it. Drip uses a finer grind of coffee than percolated—and espresso is the finest of all (a double entendre because in my opinion, it's the finest tasting too).

1 cup of espresso coffee has 350 mg of caffeine

"350 mg!! No wonder I feel so wired after an espresso from my favorite café. What about tea? Doesn't it have more caffeine than coffee?"

I have no idea where the "tea has more caffeine than coffee" myth came from, but most of the people I come across believe it. Tea has a lot less caffeine than coffee. It depends on how long you brew the tea, but even if you brew it for five minutes, it only has 40 mg of caffeine per cup versus 180 mg in drip coffee.

Maybe I should take a moment to define cup size. Whether it's coffee or tea, a cup is equivalent to a five-ounce teacup. So, if you boastfully declare, "I only drink two cups of coffee a day," but you consume drip coffee and use your favorite ten-ounce mug, that's 720 mg of caffeine a day!

•

A moderate consumption of caffeine is one five-ounce cup of drip coffee or two five-ounce cups of percolated coffee. What about instant and decaffeinated coffee?

one 5-ounce cup of instant coffee has 60 mg of caffeine
one 5-ounce cup of decaffeinated has 2 mg of caffeine

Speaking of decaffeinated coffee, is it really a better choice? It all depends on what your concerns are. For stabilizing blood sugar, hydrating your body, helping you fall asleep, and reducing your risk of osteoporosis—decaffeinated coffee is a better choice because caffeine has been found to dehydrate the body, cause insomnia, and rob calcium from your bones. But for heart disease, cancer, and fibrocystic breasts—it probably doesn't matter which you drink, regular or decaf, because moderate caffeine consumption has not been linked to heart attacks, any cancers, or painful breast lumps.

So, whatever your concerns, 200 mg of caffeine a day (one five-ounce cup of drip coffee) is considered a moderate intake. And don't forget other sources of caffeine such as soft drinks and medications.

Mountain Dew (12 oz)	54 mg	Anacin (1 tab)	32 mg
Tab (12 oz)	45 mg	Excedrin (1 tab)	65 mg
Dr Pepper (12 oz)	40 mg	Midol (1 tab)	32 mg
Pepsi (12 oz)	38 mg	Dristan (daily dose)	32 mg
Coke (12 oz)	45 mg	Dexatrim (daily dose)	200 mg
7Up (12 oz)	0 mg	Hot Chocolate (5 oz)	7 mg
Root Beer (12 oz)	0 mg	Chocolate (1 oz)	6 mg

After looking at the caffeine list, my clients are surprised by three discoveries:

•

1. Mountain Dew is higher in caffeine than Coke or Pepsi
2. Root beer contains no caffeine even though it has the cola color
3. The best surprise of all—chocolate is low in caffeine

As you know, chocolate is a top female pleasure food, and most of the women I come across are concerned about the caffeine in chocolate. No need to be too concerned; as you can see, chocolate is extremely low in caffeine—only 6 mg per ounce!

Whether it's caffeine, alcohol, or artificial sweeteners, stabilize these destabilizers by keeping your consumption to a moderate level and having them with one of your small, frequent meals. Each of these mini-meals will keep your brain energy high throughout the day—but there are certain times of the day when those small meals become most important.

10 TO 4: THE HOURS TO SAY "YES" TO FOOD CRAVINGS

I bet it was a woman who came up with the "10–4" CB radio code meaning "yes," since those are the specific hours of the day most important for fulfilling female food cravings and eating small meals. They are the hours when we should never say No and always say Yes.

Why? Because these are the times of the day when our moods and energy will be most positively affected by the foods we eat. Biological food cravings occur when the brain is open to negotiation and influence. For most women, that's between the hours of 10:00 A.M. and 4:00 P.M. Of course, it depends on what time you wake up. If you sleep until 9:59 A.M. each morning, then 10:00 A.M. to 4:00 P.M. would not be

•

your food craving hours—1:00 A.M. to 7:00 P.M. may be more like it. But for the majority of us, the body's internal clock (or the external alarm clock) rings between 6:00 and 7:00 A.M., and we begin our day.

Serotonin and the endorphins can be most significantly influenced during the midday, and that's why carbohydrates (both starch and sugar) and fat are the top female food cravings. Your female appetite is directing you toward the optimal "brain foods."

Remember: If you don't satisfy your female appetite, you'll make up for it later. If you don't satisfy your needs midmorning, you'll have stronger cravings at lunch. If you don't satisfy them at lunch, they will be even stronger midafternoon. If you don't satisfy your needs midafternoon, your cravings will be *uncontrollable* in the evening.

As a matter of fact, nighttime food cravings are most likely the product of unfulfilled food cravings during the day. Sarah was binging almost nightly because of her "Godzilla-like" food cravings; regardless of what she tried, she couldn't stop binging—until she followed the **ON** Plan and started responding to her food cravings with small meals during the day. Her nighttime binging stopped almost immediately. **If you respond to your body's food needs during the day, it doesn't need much of anything at night, except for a sound sleep.**

THE NOT-SO-IMPORTANT DINNER

"What do you mean dinner isn't important. The majority of my daily food intake is at dinner, I meet friends for dinner weekly, and I go out to dinner with my husband every Saturday night. Dinner is very important to me and my family."

The perceived importance of the dinner meal is culturally

•

driven, not biologically driven. Instead of a good-size break-fast and lunch followed by a small dinner, we have forced our bodies to eat the direct opposite of what they naturally need. The modern day work ethic is responsible. Most people have a long commute in the morning, a thirty-minute lunch break, and no snack breaks. The only chance we get to feed our bodies is from the time we get home until the time we go to bed.

You may think dinner is important, but as far as your metabolism, weight, energy levels, and moods are concerned—dinner is the least important meal because:

- Your brain chemicals are functioning on their own *as long as you* fulfilled your needs during the day.
- Your body's metabolism is quickly declining and needs very few calories to function.

During the first twelve hours of the day, your body and brain need the most energy and nutrients to function. If you wake up at 6:00 A.M. each morning, for the first twelve hours of your day until 6:00 P.M., your body and brain are working overtime. Your metabolism and body temperature are at their highest levels and you are burning hundreds and hundreds of calories. Your brain is in the "let's get things done" mode and will be as long as you feed it with your female pleasure foods and a stable blood sugar supply.

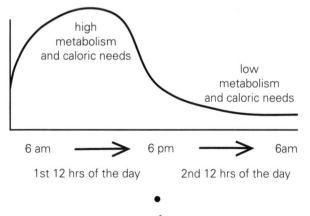

But after 6:00 P.M., you're lucky if your body needs 400 calories to function. How many calories do you give it? 800 calories? 1,000 calories? 1,500 calories?

Most women eat about 1,000 calories after 6:00 P.M.— that's 600 calories more than what their bodies need to function for the next twelve hours until waking up the following morning. Where do those excess calories go? You guessed it—straight to the thighs. **What you eat at night is not for your brain or body, it's for your fat cells.**

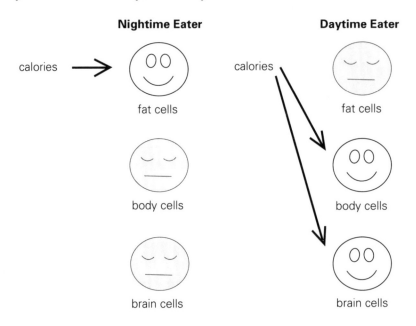

Your body and brain really don't need dinner; they require only the evening snack. If you were at a restaurant and let your brain do the ordering, it would decide on an appetizer instead of the all-you-can-eat buffet.

If you don't eat during the day, you are setting yourself up for a big dinner despite any efforts to eat less. Your brain and body are saying, "Hey! I need to make up for what you didn't

•

give me over the last twelve hours." Your appetite is equivalent to a bear's, you nibble all night long trying to satisfy your unmet needs, and your stomach is overflowing when you retire for the night. Then, the next day, you repeat the same behavior: You don't eat during the day and you are famished when you get home at night.

What's the first room in the house you walk into when you get home from the day's activities? Any chance it's the kitchen? Ninety-four percent of us head straight for the kitchen without even thinking about it. Now, maybe your door opens into the kitchen and you have no choice, but what do you do in the kitchen?

Sally used to skip lunch and be absolutely starving when she walked through the door. She would make a beeline for the kitchen and vacuum out a couple of cupboards plus a shelf in the refrigerator. Then, she would nibble while preparing dinner, eat a four-course dinner, and snack while watching TV. She couldn't understand why she was tired during the day and gaining weight.

Then the light bulb of understanding flashed on. "It makes so much sense to me now. I have been eating the direct opposite of my biological needs and have let dinner dominate my eating habits. No wonder I feel exhausted all the time, have mood swings like a giant pendulum, and have been fighting a weight problem unsuccessfully for most of my life. I can't wait to stop emphasizing dinner and start emphasizing my midday meals."

I hope it makes sense to you too so that you are motivated to match your eating to your metabolism and use food to your biological advantage. **Daytime calories will be burned, nighttime calories will be stored.**

If you eat a lot at night, you are activating your fat cells. The five-course meal you ate last night will be found some-

•

where in your fat cells the next morning. Once it's in there, it's there for good—unless you exercise.

"What about exercise? If I exercised at night, wouldn't that boost my metabolism so that I could eat more at dinner without gaining weight?" Many of my clients ask this question, and it is true that exercise boosts your metabolism, but the effects are long-term, not short-term. It boosts metabolism all day long, not just right after you exercise. Scheduling your workout at night might help a little, but I would rather see you make your dinner smaller and exercise when it is convenient for you.

Emphasize your midday meals and de-emphasize dinner. Easy to say, but sometimes difficult to put into practice. The large dinner meal and overeating at night have become so ingrained in our culture that we think we need it.

I need something sweet at night—By satisfying your needs during the day, you'll most likely find that you don't need anything sweet at night. If you are responding to your body's needs during the day, but still crave something sweet at night, first make sure that it is not an emotional craving; if it is indeed a biological craving, satisfy it with a very small amount.

I need food to help me relax at night—Eating is not an effective relaxation technique. It's so ineffective that often the result is even greater stress because we feel guilty and start to worry about weight gain. Wouldn't something else be more effective to help you relax? Reading a book, listening to music, drinking some herbal tea?

I need to eat right before bed to help me fall asleep—Using food to induce slumber is deceiving. The blood directed to your stomach for digestion may make your brain sleepy, but you'll have a more fitful, less restful sleep. If you have difficulty falling asleep, the next chapter will provide some effective techniques.

•

I need to eat a large dinner with my family—All family members would probably benefit from a smaller dinner, but if they are not amenable to it, serve them larger portions, yourself smaller portions—and enjoy the family time. Even if you eat a smaller dinner three or four nights a week, you'll notice the benefits.

There is no physiological need to eat more than a mini-meal at night. Most other cultures eat their biggest meal midday, and they do not have the weight problems we do. Nor, coincidentally, do they have the severity of PMS and menopausal symptoms. We are designed to eat small frequent meals—with the smallest of them all at night.

STOP! ARE YOU EXPERIENCING A BIOLOGICAL FEMALE FOOD CRAVING RIGHT NOW?

If the answer is yes, check the time of the day to see if it is during your female food craving hours of 10:00 A.M. to 4:00 P.M. and make it a part of one of your five small meals for the day.

Now that you have all the knowledge and skills to Distribute Your Food to Maximize Mood, let's put this next step into practice.

•

WEEK 4:   Your **ON** Action Plan

STEP 4:   Distribute Your Food to Maximize Mood

GOALS:
1. Eat 5 small meals a day to stabilize blood sugar.
2. Stabilize the blood sugar destabilizers.
3. Focus on the midday hours to balance brain chemicals.
4. Emphasize lunch and de-emphasize dinner.

TECHNIQUES:
1. Divide your food up into mini-meals.
2. Split your sandwich at lunch.
3. Keep snacks in your purse or glove compartment.
4. Prepare a grocery list of easy snacks.
5. Keep some food in your office.
6. Consume sugar, caffeine, alcohol, and artificial sweeteners with a small meal.
7. Moderate your intake of caffeine, alcohol, and artificial sweeteners.
8. Pay close attention to food cravings during the hours of 10 A.M. to 4 P.M.
9. Think of your dinner meal as your evening snack.
10. Realize that a large dinner leads to weight gain.
11. Use the Hunger/Fullness Rating Scale.
12. Use the Mood Scale.
13. Keep eating records for the next week to practice these techniques.

•

For this fourth week, I still want you to assess your hunger, mood state before and after eating, level of fullness, and level of satisfaction, but I also want you to begin focusing on distributing your food intake in small meals with special emphasis on the hours between 10 A.M. and 4 P.M. Record the time you ate your small meal or snack, whether or not you were experiencing a food craving, and don't forget to watch out for food-mood competition and the blood sugar destabilizers.

On the following pages are a sample eating record and a blank record to use for the next week. This is your final one!

•

EATING RECORD FOR DISTRIBUTING FOOD

Time	Meal/ Snack Food Craving	Hunger Level	Mood State	Compe- tition? Desta- bilizers?	Fullness Level	Mood State	Satis- faction
___	___	___	___	___	___	___	___
	___			___			
	___			___			
___	___	___	___	___	___	___	___
	___			___			
	___			___			
___	___	___	___	___	___	___	___
	___			___			
	___			___			
___	___	___	___	___	___	___	___
	___			___			
	___			___			
___	___	___	___	___	___	___	___
	___			___			
	___			___			
___	___	___	___	___	___	___	___
	___			___			
	___			___			
___	___	___	___	___	___	___	___
	___			___			
	___			___			
___	___	___	___	___	___	___	___
	___			___			
	___			___			
___	___	___	___	___	___	___	___
	___			___			
	___			___			

•

EATING RECORD FOR DISTRIBUTING FOOD

Time	Meal/ Snack Food Craving	Hunger Level	Mood State	Compe- tition? Desta- bilizers?	Fullness Level	Mood State	Satis- faction
___	___	___	___	___	___	___	___
	___			___			
	___			___			
___	___	___	___	___	___	___	___
	___			___			
	___			___			
___	___	___	___	___	___	___	___
	___			___			
	___			___			
___	___	___	___	___	___	___	___
	___			___			
	___			___			
___	___	___	___	___	___	___	___
	___			___			
	___			___			
___	___	___	___	___	___	___	___
	___			___			
	___			___			
___	___	___	___	___	___	___	___
	___			___			
	___			___			

•

Eight

P AT YOURSELF ON THE BACK, give yourself a high five, treat yourself to a piece of chocolate. You have uncovered your optimal eating routine! You have stripped away the ancient nutritional beliefs and the old unhealthy eating rules, you have buried all the diet programs and food plans, and you have let your body define the whats, whys, and whens of healthy eating. Changing your attitudes, beliefs, and behaviors is not an easy task. Be proud of your accomplishments.

Theresa reflected on the last four weeks. "When I first started the **ON** Plan, I thought that it was going to be like a rerun of 'Mission Impossible.' It sounded too good to be true—eat what you want and crave, listen to your body's hunger and fullness signals, and you will stabilize mood, revitalize energy, and lose weight *while* eating chocolate? But in just four weeks, I feel better than I have ever felt in my life, my period came and went without the usual stampede of buffalos that announces its arrival, and I've lost a couple of pounds without even trying."

•

I hope that you have had similar experiences. Look how far you've come over the last month. Before reading this book, you were trying to fight your female food cravings through denial, elimination, and restriction—but that battle was eventually lost with an inevitable binge. You were skipping meals during the day, overeating dinner at night, and your weight, moods, mind, and body were bearing the brunt of your less than optimal eating routine.

Now—with the guidance of the **ON** Plan and your intuitive food awareness—you are feeding your female body and mind to maximize your moods and benefit your body as never before.

The ON Plan

trust and fulfill your food cravings

de-emphasize dinner   Mood   eat chocolate in moderation

emphasize lunch   Minimizing   eat sugar in moderation
                       Body

eat 5 small meals a day   Benefiting   eat fat in moderation

focus on starches

You've gained the trust to fulfill your food cravings with a moderate amount of what you crave. You've realized how vital food satisfaction is and how to achieve it. You've also realized how important small meals, snacking, and lunch are to the female body and mind. Now, the next step is to follow your optimal eating routine and to use it to your rhythmic advantage—daily, monthly, and yearly; and particularly when your brain is under significant strain with too much stress or too little sleep.

•

OPTIMAL EATING FOR YOUR DAILY RHYTHMS

Your body and brain work on natural daily cycles with fluctuations in brain chemicals, blood glucose levels, hormones, body temperature, and metabolic rate. You are a "diurnal" being which means that your body works on a day/night cycle and all of your body's processes are timed to keep you awake and functioning during the day and asleep and resting during the night.

These cycles occur every twenty-four hours and are precisely synchronized by a special timepiece in your brain called the Suprachiasmatic Nucleus. Although it sounds like something Mary Poppins should be singing about, it's the home of your internal biological clock. That clock does more than "tick away" your fertile years, it also ticks, times, and coordinates all of your bodily processes.

Your body is like a 10,000 piece orchestra and your brain is the conductor. All of the body's instruments need to be synchronized to produce the best sounding music. What you eat and when you eat can either make them harmonize or go off-key. When you eat in accordance with your daily biological needs, you are in harmony with your body's rhythms. The **ON** Plan turns on your optimal daily rhythms and uses food to your rhythmic advantage so that you function at a level of maximum efficiency during the day and achieve a level of maximum deep sleep at night.

You may not realize it, but you are already following your optimal daily eating routine and using food to your rhythmic advantage. But let me give you even more persuasive information as to why you will want to follow the **ON** Plan every day for the rest of your life.

During the day, your body and brain are pumped up and need to be constantly fueled by specific foods dictated by your

•

food cravings. But at night, your body and brain are slowing down and preparing for sleep; therefore, they don't need much of anything.

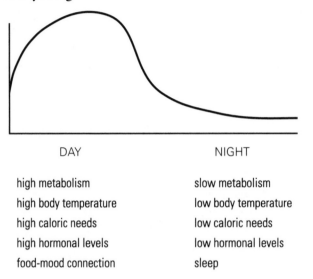

DAY	NIGHT
high metabolism	slow metabolism
high body temperature	low body temperature
high caloric needs	low caloric needs
high hormonal levels	low hormonal levels
food-mood connection	sleep

Your body's rhythms wake you up in the morning and keep you up and functioning during the day, therefore, your optimal eating routine logically starts with breakfast.

Breakfast—Your Body's Wake-Up Call

The sun rises in the morning and the world wakes up. Your body's alarm clock rings with a surge of hormones, brain chemicals, and biochemical stimulants. What's best to break the fast and start the day off right with synchronized rhythms? The answer is carbohydrates; not for brain serotonin, but for your body.

You've fasted for the last ten to twelve hours since your last meal, which hopefully was really an evening snack. Overnight, your caloric needs, as low as they were, were met from glucose stores in your muscle and liver. When you wake up in

•

the morning, your body's first goal is to replenish those glucose stores, and your brain releases a chemical that leads you toward high-carbohydrate foods to accomplish this goal. This chemical is called neuropeptide Y, and it is your body's wake-up call for carbohydrates.

It's no coincidence that the traditional breakfast staples are foods like cereal, toast, pancakes, waffles, and pastries. Even before the discovery of neuropeptide Y, our bodies naturally had an affinity for starch and sugar in the morning. Food companies have seized the opportunity to market appealing breakfast foods like donuts, bear claws, almond croissants, cream puffs, and cheese danish.

When you walk into a bakery in the morning and your eyes gaze at these high-sugar foods, the neuropeptide Y causes your mouth to water. These foods will replenish the glucose stores in your muscle and liver, but (as you know from previous chapters) they will also negatively affect your blood sugar levels, and hence lower your morning stamina. For example, if you eat a donut and wash it down with a cup of coffee, within an hour or so, you may feel compelled to crawl back under the covers.

So, what's the breakfast of champions? Start the day with high-starch foods and respond to the messages from neuropeptide Y to replenish your carbohydrate stores without depleting your blood sugar. Some people report that including protein also helps to jump start their day. There is no need to worry about food-mood competition in the morning.

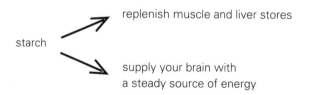

starch → replenish muscle and liver stores
starch → supply your brain with a steady source of energy

•

"But what if I'm not hungry in the morning? Should I force myself to eat breakfast?" I get this question over and over again, and I usually respond by asking some important questions.

- What did you eat for dinner last night?
- Did you snack after dinner?
- Did you eat before going to bed?

Because your stomach is also trying to get some shut-eye, little digestion occurs during sleep, so if you ate a five-course dinner meal, or had three ice cream bars while watching TV, or had a triple-decker club sandwich with a side of chips before bed (or all of the above), you'll wake up in the morning with some food still left in your stomach. How could you be hungry?

Actually, one of the best signs that you have achieved an optimal eating routine is that you *are* hungry first thing in the morning. If you've followed the **ON** Plan and had a small dinner, your stomach will be eager for food in the morning, and neuropeptide Y will stimulate food cravings for carbohydrates to replenish your stores.

small dinner → hungry → neuropeptide → starch
last night   this morning   Y   cravings

Sally was concerned that something was amiss with her eating routine. Although she was eating small, frequent meals and a dinner meal half its former size, she still wasn't hungry in the morning. "The thought of food before 9:00 A.M. makes me nauseous. I know that I'm not pregnant, so it can't be morning sickness. What's the matter with me?" Nothing was the matter with her or with you if "morning food sickness" is

•

something that plagues you. Everybody's optimal eating routine works a bit differently. If you are following the **ON** Plan but are still not hungry first thing in the morning, then listen to your body and don't eat. If your body sends you signals at 9:00 A.M., then eat at 9:00 A.M. Just don't make the common mistake of not eating anything until lunch (the next socially accepted mealtime). By that time, you'll be overhungry, wind up overeating, and then cause even more disruption in your daily rhythms.

"Tell me exactly what I should be eating for breakfast." My seminar attendees and my clients always request specifics, and they are disappointed when I turn the tables and ask them to tell me what they need. I can't tell them or you what to eat for breakfast or any other meal. **Only *your* body can tell you what it needs.** Based on daily biological rhythms and neuropeptide Y, I *can* tell you that most likely your body is directing you toward starch and maybe some protein, but the type of starch and what you eat along with it is up to you. And it can change daily. Today you may have needed cereal and milk, tomorrow a soft-boiled egg on toast, and the day after leftover pasta.

Midmorning Mood Munchies

Let's say you responded to your body's wake-up call for carbohydrates first thing in the morning, and you ate a moderate amount of carbos with perhaps some protein or fruit. You felt productive throughout the first few hours of the day, but now it's three hours later, and if you are responding to your body's biological rhythms, you should feel hungry again and may start to feel a drop in energy and mood. Your optimal eating routine anticipates your needs and fulfills them at the perfect time; your midmorning snack will give you the lift you need for the rest of the morning.

•

What are the best midmorning mood snacks to lift your mood?

Again, there is no "best"; just choose whatever you *want* and *crave*—and for the first time of the day, you may be craving something that will enhance not only your brain sugar supply but also your brain chemicals and mood. Remember the hours to say "yes" to food cravings: 10:00 A.M. to 4:00 P.M. Late morning is when your brain chemicals can be positively influenced by food. Occasionally you may desire protein for a dopamine release, but nine times out of ten, it will be carbohydrates—not to replenish your glucose stores, but this time to revitalize your body and mind by balancing brain serotonin and blood sugar.

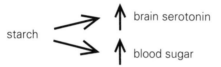

A Lunch to Launch Your Moods

You've felt great all morning because your breakfast and midmorning snack were synchronized with your biological rhythms. Now you are starting to get hungry again. Before your blood sugar and brain chemicals drop too low, it's time to fuel those rhythms.

Each of the five small meals a day is important to the female body and mind, but midday is when all of your metabolic processes are functioning at the highest possible levels—and this is why lunch will launch your moods, energy, and productivity for the rest of the day.

•

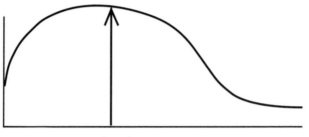

Lunch

"Is this that power lunch thing that everyone is talking about?" You can call it that, but this power lunch is designed only for women—to balance their brain chemicals and blood sugar. A "power lunch" for women focuses on the specific foods that her body is requesting.

Sometimes your body may ask for protein, so the power lunch may be a chicken breast or a roast beef sandwich. However, most of the time you'll probably find that your body is demanding carbohydrates for the calming effects of serotonin. If that's the case, your power lunch would be mostly carbohydrates, vegetables, and maybe a little fat. If you eat too much protein with the carbohydrate, you wouldn't get the boost in serotonin that you need because protein competes—and wins.

"I've been listening to my cravings and eating pasta with tomato sauce almost every day at lunch, but within a half hour I feel a post-lunch dip instead of an afternoon power surge." Jessica thought that maybe starches weren't her longtime companion. As it turned out, the reason her pasta lunch wasn't giving the expected explosion of energy was because of the amount she was eating. Her luncheon plate of pasta looked like a mountain range; instead of climbing it, she ate it.

Overeating overloads the brain. If you overeat lunch (even one that's mostly carbohydrates), your brain goes into overload, and blood is shunted away from it to the stomach to

•

carry out the lengthy digestive process. Your brain's sugar and nutrient supply are cut off, so it cuts off your energy.

If, instead, you listen to your female needs, and feed your body with a moderate amount at lunch, the afternoon forecast would read "clear, crisp thinking for the remainder of the day with a sunny disposition." If you overate or skipped lunch, the afternoon forecast would read "cloudy thinking for the rest of the afternoon with turbulent and overcast moods."

Eat to Beat the 3:30 P.M. Slump

As you move through the day and arrive at midafternoon, you are starting to feel hungry again with your moods and energy in need of a lift.

Somewhere between the hours of 2:00 and 4:00 P.M., the infamous afternoon slump occurs and we experience a drop in mood, energy, and productivity. Some chronobiologists (experts in biological rhythms) believe that we are all biologically designed to nap in the afternoon. Many cultures do. They have siestas, and in the afternoon all business ceases for a couple of hours. When we travel abroad, many of us have a difficult time understanding this practice and are often disappointed when we find that shopping time has been significantly limited. These cultures, however, do not have the obesity problem we do, nor do they experience the high risk for stress-related diseases.

Our work schedules have prevented us from napping in the afternoon, so instead we fight the urge with sugar and caffeine. They may increase energy, but only for a short while, after which energy levels drop even lower than before the doses of sugar and caffeine.

Whether or not the afternoon slump is a message from our biological clocks to nap, some brain chemical changes take place that do reduce energy and stimulate cravings for certain foods. These brain chemical changes explain why we

•

are likely to spend more money on chocolate in the afternoon than at any other time during the day.

The main reason for this afternoon chocolate urge is another female brain chemical—galanin. Don't worry, it's the last one! In the late afternoon, your brain releases galanin, and your appetite leads you toward high-fat foods. Galanin stimulates your fat cravings *and* stimulates the storage of fat in your fat cells.

"Why on earth would my brain want to do a thing like that? I don't want to crave fat and I certainly don't want to store fat and gain weight." Your brain has a mind of its own, and a reason for everything it does. The explanation for this goes back to the female survival mechanism. Metabolism and caloric needs significantly drop in the afternoon, so with galanin the brain uses this opportunity to store as much fat as possible to prepare for famine.

The powers that control the female appetite are vast and strong. You can't prevent the galanin release (sorry, there is no anti-galanin pill yet, although laboratories are working on it), and you can't fight the fat cravings, but by satisfying them immediately with a *small amount* and by exercising regularly (coming up in the next chapter), you can subdue them.

If you satisfy the craving with a very small amount of fat, galanin will feel as if it accomplished its afternoon goal and will willingly retreat until tomorrow afternoon. But, if you try to resist the fat cravings, galanin will be released in full force, and you'll crave more fat throughout the rest of the day.

So, what's best to beat the afternoon slump? Again, it's whatever *you* are craving, but based on afternoon brain chemistry, a little sugar, a little starch, and a little fat might just do the trick.

sugar—for the quick energy burst you need to get you out of the slump

•

starch—to maintain the positive energy throughout the rest of the day

fat—to respond to the request of galanin and also to increase endorphins for mood enhancement

(Some examples of afternoon stamina snacks are: a bran or blueberry muffin, a piece of chocolate with a couple of crackers, or a half a bagel with a little cream cheese and a glass of juice.)

Galanin and the endorphins work together. Galanin stimulates fat cravings and after we eat the fat, the endorphins give us the positive reinforcement for making a wise decision by making us feel good. When we respond to our fat cravings by eating a small amount, a positive mood appears and the craving disappears.

galanin → ↑ fat cravings → eat fat ↗ ↑ endorphins → ↑ mood
↘ ↓ galanin → ↓ fat craving

Another benefit of the late afternoon snack is that it will reduce cravings as well as the amount you need to eat at night. You won't be starving when you walk in the door, and you won't need to head straight into the kitchen.

As we discussed in depth in the last chapter, because your body and brain don't really need to be fueled after 6:00 P.M., dinner is the least important meal of the day. At night, your metabolism-stimulating brain chemicals punch the clock, and your sleep-inducing brain chemicals report to work. Neither your brain nor your body needs much food at night. This is the perfect opportunity to focus on other foods for good health: a substantial protein source along with milk products.

Let's put your daily biochemical food needs all together.

•

Breakfast	Morning Snack	Lunch	Afternoon Snack	Dinner
Neuropeptide Y	serotonin	serotonin or dopamine	galanin endorphins serotonin	∅
↓	↓	↓	↓	↓
carbos (and maybe some protein)	carbos	carbos or protein	carbos and fat	protein and calcium

fast metabolism ⟶ slow metabolism

Of course, vegetables can and should be eaten at any time throughout the day! Remember: What's most important is that you listen to your food messages. If the afternoon message is to eat yogurt or the dinner message is to eat pasta—then eat them!

This *is* the optimal daily eating routine that your body will naturally want to follow. It matches and complements your daily female biorhythms by eating the right foods at the right times. But there are two other natural female rhythms to tell you about.

USING FOOD TO YOUR RHYTHMIC ADVANTAGE—MONTHLY AND YEARLY

Your monthly rhythms are influenced by hormonal fluctuations, and your yearly rhythms are influenced by seasonal changes. These rhythms are really not much different from your daily rhythms. They reflect the highs and the lows in hormonal fluctuations, metabolism, energy, and mood.

•

184

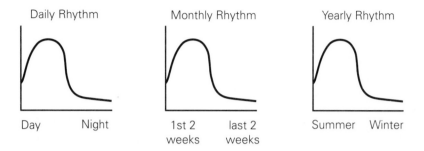

During the high point of the month and the year, you feel your best and you have the most energy. When the rhythm dips premenstrually and during the winter months, your optimal eating routine is *necessary* to keep your moods, mind, and energy balanced.

"If I follow my optimal eating routine, will it cure my PMS?" PMS cannot be cured because it is not a disease. I will not promise that your symptoms will disappear with the **ON** Plan, but they will become more manageable. Some monthly changes are inevitable and a natural part of being a woman.

Just as women experience mood changes and food cravings at certain times of the day (10:00 A.M. to 4:00 P.M.), we also experience them at certain times of the month—the last two weeks of our menstrual cycle. Eighty-seven percent of the women I surveyed reported having increased food cravings premenstrually. The week or so before we start our periods, all the daily changes and cravings become more apparent.

- We have stronger food cravings from 10 A.M. to 4 P.M.
- We crave more chocolate, sugar, and fat.
- We have a more pronounced drop in afternoon energy.
- We have more significant mood swings.
- We are more affected by the highs and lows of blood sugar.

Therefore, listening and responding to our body's food needs is vital. **Premenstrual food cravings are Mother Na-**

•

ture's solution to stabilizing mood and revitalizing energy. As women begin the perimenopausal transition, these monthly changes heighten. In fact, one of the first signs that we have begun the transition is increased premenstrual tension.

"You mean it's going to get worse than this?" Sabrina was thirty-nine years old and had noticed that her premenstrual tension had increased over the last couple of years. As it turned out, her PMS wasn't going to get any worse because she was already in the transition to menopause. This transition begins at various times for women, but it appears to be starting earlier and lasting longer. Whatever the explanation may be for this change—stress, the environment, or poor lifestyle habits—responding to your food cravings becomes even more important!

During the transition to menopause, food cravings may become stronger and more frequent, mood swings more dramatic. If you are a premenopausal woman reading this book, it is my hope that with your optimal eating routine in place, you will minimize the changes during perimenopause. If you are already in the transition as you are reading this, it's never too late. Use food to your rhythmic advantage, and commit to trusting and responding to your body's needs.

After the transition is over and you have entered the post-menopausal years, the monthly rhythms are more like small ripples in the water instead of tidal waves. It was interesting to observe from the results of my survey how food cravings change for the postmenopausal woman.

- There is a significant reduction in sugar and fat cravings—**but not chocolate cravings!!**
- There is a significant increase in protein, vegetable, and fruit cravings.

•

Postmenopausally, estrogen and the other female hormones are no longer fluctuating and affecting one's brain chemicals and body rhythms. So the biological need for sugar and fat diminishes. Postmenopausal women are also not as sensitive to blood sugar changes. Small, frequent meals are still important for weight control, but they aren't as important for stabilizing blood sugar.

What explains the more frequent protein cravings? All women have some testosterone; after menopause, testosterone starts to have more of an influence on a woman's body, including her food cravings. In addition, as we all grow older, the need for protein to maintain muscle mass and fruits and vegetables to provide nutrients starts to take priority.

With hormone replacement therapy, the external source of estrogen will stimulate sugar and fat cravings once again. Hormone replacement therapy offers many benefits, but it's important to anticipate how it will affect your food cravings.

Your optimal eating routine is important for the monthly cycles during the premenopausal and perimenopausal years. But, regardless of menstrual status, yearly changes that are influenced by the seasons also take place in appetite and food cravings.

As new research on the food-mood connection continues to surface, almost everything can be explained by changes in brain chemicals. The shorter daylight hours of the winter affect many hormones and brain chemicals, including your brain serotonin levels. The fewer the number of daylight hours, the lower your brain serotonin levels, the more negative your moods, and the more you crave carbohydrates to balance your brain chemicals and mood.

•

Women are more sensitive to changes in brain serotonin levels to begin with, and that's why we are six times more likely than men to experience Seasonal Affective Disorder (appropriately abbreviated SAD), the extreme effect of the winter months. With SAD, the mood changes are severe enough to interfere with our daily functioning because the body's rhythms and brain chemicals are thrown out of whack in the winter, then balance out again in the summer. However, there are varying degrees of seasonal changes, and the lesser version is called "winter doldrums" or "winter blues."

Light has a positive effect on serotonin, and that's why we have more energy, fewer PMS and menopausal symptoms, and fewer food cravings during the summer months. In the winter, however, as the days start to shorten, serotonin levels drop, and we feel more fatigued and stressed, and have stronger PMS and menopausal symptoms. *And* we crave more carbohydrates. As a matter of fact, research has shown that on average we consume 500 more calories a day from carbohydrates in January than in July.

	Summer Months	Winter Months
average number of daylight hours	14 hrs	10 hrs
brain serotonin levels	increase	decrease
mood state	positive	negative
energy level	increased	decreased
PMS and menopausal symptoms	decreased	increased
carbohydrate cravings	decreased	increased

The winter carbohydrate cravings are an instinctive message to balance the serotonin levels that have been disrupted by darkness. In line with the message throughout this book: *Trust them and respond to them!*

In addition to fulfilling your carbohydrate cravings, there are some other ways to take care of yourself during the winter

•

months. How about scheduling a trip to a sunnier climate each winter? It's not a bad idea, and it's often recommended as part of the treatment for Seasonal Affective Disorder. Here are some other suggestions:

- Try to get at least half an hour of natural outdoor light each day.
- Install a skylight.
- Move closer to the Equator (couldn't resist!).
- Investigate light therapy, a special device with high-intensity light that has been found to be extremely effective in treating Seasonal Affective Disorder, reducing depression, and tempering premenstrual and menopausal tension. Talk to your doctor about it.

An understandable yearly pattern pertains to mood changes and food cravings as the daylight hours decline in the winter months. Not surprisingly, there is also a yearly pattern to weight gain and loss. No doubt you've experienced it, so I'm not telling you anything new by saying we weigh more in the winter months than in the summer months. On average, most people gain about eight pounds in the winter. A number of explanations have been offered for this winter weight gain.

1. **The Hibernation Reaction** We are biologically programmed to increase stored fat in preparation for the winter months. Are we also programmed to crawl into a cave and sleep for three months? For those who live in colder climates, there may be a need to keep the body warm with increased insulation from additional body fat, but then again these days we also have down parkas, central heating, and fireplaces.
2. **The Carbohydrate Calorie Theory** Because we crave more carbohydrates to balance serotonin, we are eating

•

more calories and gaining more weight. But if we immediately respond to those cravings with a small amount when we are hungry, the carbohydrate cravings shouldn't cause any weight gain at all. If we deny those cravings, the end result is overeating—and the overeating leads to an overweight body. This theory holds true only if we are not responding to our instinctive food needs.

3. **The Holiday Factor**   Is it the hibernation reaction, the carbohydrate calorie theory—or is it the six weeks of family dinners, parties, eggnog, Christmas cookies, vacations away from home, and a vacation away from exercise? Almost all of that eight-pound winter weight gain takes place between Thanksgiving and New Year's. During the holidays, we are eating more, exercising less—and our fat cells are having more of a holiday celebration than we are. I vote for this theory.

The **ON** Plan will help you prevent the winter weight gain and minimize seasonal changes in energy and mood. **Your optimal eating routine anticipates the changes in brain chemicals and balances your rhythms before they create an imbalance in your life.**

Besides these natural daily, monthly, and yearly rhythmic changes, other factors can disrupt your rhythms and cause your body to get off beat and your brain out of synch. Just as a piano needs to be tuned each year or a car needs a tune-up every 20,000 miles, sometimes your brain is under so much strain that it, too, requires a tune-up.

WHEN YOUR BRAIN IS UNDER STRAIN

"What do you mean *when* my brain is under strain; my brain is always under strain, from the moment I wake up until the moment I go to bed. I'm a single mother with three kids who is getting her master's at night and working full-time during the day."

For many of us, brain strain is an all too common occurrence. Simply trying to function on a day-to-day basis can cause brain strain. Brain strain is when some external force has upset your body's balance and disrupted your biological rhythms. The two most disruptive sources of brain strain for women are too much stress and too little sleep.

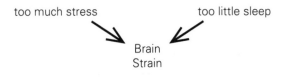

Each of these circumstances affects the balance of brain chemicals and thus the balance of our lives. They can make our food cravings stronger and more frequent—but we can also use food during these times to balance our brains and synchronize our rhythms.

Stress—a Pain in the Brain

Hundreds of books have been written on stress, most of them focused either on the negative effects of stress on heart disease and other diseases or on managing the stress through effective coping skills. Well, an added bonus of the **ON** Plan is that it is a highly effective stress management technique.

Unfortunately, when we are under stress, our commitment to healthful eating can easily get buried beneath the growing pile of things to do, problems to solve, and demands to deal with. All of a sudden, we forget about the importance of fulfilling our female food cravings and eating five small meals a day. We skip meals, we rely on fast food, we seek out sugar and caffeine to keep us going. Our first impulse is to go

•

off the **ON** Plan . . . **DON'T!** Let that impulse pass and make a stronger commitment to stay on the **ON** Plan.

To explain fully why the **ON** Plan is especially important when you are under stress, let's first look at your body's physiological response to stress and how it stresses your rhythms.

Your body is programmed to save your life when you are under stress. We all know it as the fight-or-flight response. This response originated from the life-threatening stressors placed on us thousands of years ago: fighting against an animal or an enemy and fleeing as fast as possible. Your body aids you by providing extra energy, concentration, and strength in life-threatening situations. You may not participate in physical combat very often or have to run for your life from an angry saber-toothed tiger, but the same reactions occur today with a saber-toothed boss, a mammoth spouse, killer deadlines, combative commuter traffic, and fiendish financial worries. You may wish you could flee and run away from it all, but that is usually not an acceptable option. Your body, however, is still triggering lifesaving biochemical changes, and what was a protective mechanism yesterday is causing us problems today.

Adrenaline, the stress hormone, causes a cascade of reactions to accomplish three goals:

1. to mobilize immediate energy for strength and endurance
2. to increase alertness and quicken reaction time
3. to prevent injury, blood loss, and death

In case you need to fight or flee, glucose is released from the stores in your muscle and liver, and blood is directed to your major muscle groups. Your heart rate and blood pressure increase, your breathing increases, and your blood glu-

•

cose increases. Now your muscles and cardiovascular system are fully prepared to put up a fight or to flee.

Your brain is also preparing to help you focus on the life-threatening situation through an increase in the supply of brain glucose and brain chemicals to make you more alert to the environment, focused on your surroundings, and clear in your thinking.

Just in case your muscles and brain don't completely protect you, your body's final mechanism for survival is to prevent death from injury and blood loss. Clotting factors are released to minimize blood loss during a potential injury.

Once the stressful situation is over, your body goes into the recovery phase and all the variables are decreased as the body tries to restore itself.

> decreased blood sugar
> decreased brain glucose supply
> decreased brain chemicals

This recovery period is when you experience overwhelming fatigue, mood swings, lack of concentration, and the need for slumber. This time is also when you experience food cravings. Your brain chemicals are reduced, your muscles want to replenish their glucose stores, and your blood sugar is low. No wonder most people report sugar cravings when they have been under stress. The body perceives sugar as a quick way to recover from stress.

As a matter of fact, sugar cravings are built into the word stress. Look at the word *stressed* and spell it backward. No wonder we go for desserts during these times.

The most stress I have ever been under was during the Oakland Hills fire. With 100-foot flames 500 feet away and no fire trucks in sight, I thank God for the stress response.

•

Although I'm the type of person who would more likely lose her cool during an emergency, my brain and body took over to do what had to be done. My mind was focused on gathering irreplaceable, precious belongings (and remembering where they were). My body was equipped with the strength and endurance to move quickly, pack up the car, and flee. Then after it was over, and we were safely at a friend's house (we were among the lucky few whose homes were spared), the recovery phase set in. Emotions surfaced. I could barely remember my name, I wanted sugar, and I wanted to fall into a deep sleep. But during the fire, when I needed all of my faculties, the stress response made sure that I was working at 100 percent efficiency.

There may be occasions such as mine when we need the stress response for its warriorlike purpose. The problem is that the same response occurs whether it's a fire or getting fired. You may need the positive brain changes, but you don't need the muscular and cardiovascular changes—and this is when the **ON** Plan is particularly effective.

The **ON** Plan can turn on relaxation, calmness, and mood stability during the stress response and the recovery phase. Ideally, it would be best to eliminate some of the sources of stress in our lives. You could change your occupation to one that is lower on the stress list. Have you ever thought of becoming a gardener or a librarian? You could move to a less stressed country. Have you ever thought of moving to France? You could let go of some responsibilities. Have you ever thought of hiding in a cave for a week? Getting to the source of the stress is most effective, but not always realistic. Your optimal eating routine is an effective, realistic solution that you can use every day.

Some level of stress is necessary to get us going in the morning. If we didn't have any lists of things to do, goals to accomplish, or challenges to meet, we would be reluctant to

•

crawl out of bed. The reality of our lives is that a certain amount of stress is positive; too much stress is negative. Where it crosses the line differs for each of us. It's like a violin: If the strings are too loose, you won't like the music; if the strings are too tight, they may break. When you are wound up too tight, you are in a state of anxiety and don't sleep well at night.

Sleep Deprivation—Your Brain Needs a Good Night's Sleep

We have all experienced sleep deprivation from time to time, and for some, it may be all the time. You may have flown across the country or across an ocean, have a newborn at home, be studying for a test, working late at night, working the night shift, or trying to meet your manuscript deadline (as I am doing right now). Or you have a sleep disorder that is causing chronic sleep deprivation.

If you've experienced sleep deprivation, then you've also experienced the negative effects on mood, concentration, energy level, reaction time, food cravings, and general well-being.

The sleep/wake cycle is the most important of all your biological rhythms. It synchronizes every single system in your body, including your brain. If your sleep/wake cycle is off, so are your brain function and brain chemical levels.

Not surprisingly, women are three times more likely to experience insomnia and other sleep difficulties than men. One of the most important sleep-inducing brain chemicals is none other than serotonin, and as you have read many times in this book, women are more sensitive to drops in serotonin. That's why we experience daily food cravings, monthly and seasonal changes, and stress-related sugar cravings. That's why sleep difficulties become even more prevalent premenstrually and menopausally. The decline in estrogen affects the

•

sleep cycles, and the night sweats can cause one to awaken in a pool of sweat.

"I'm confused. Does serotonin cause enhanced mood or cause sleepiness?" It is confusing, because nighttime and day-time serotonin are different. Balanced daytime serotonin makes you feel calm, productive, and energized, but the sero-tonin released at night is a signal that it's time for slumber. It's the sprinkling of sleep sand that leads us under the covers.

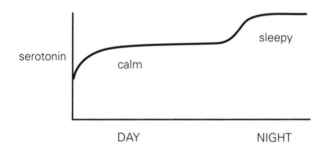

Sleep is restorative to the body and mind and keeps your daily rhythms in synch. Sleep deprivation throws off your rhythms and you may crave more sugar, fat, and chocolate as your body tries to recapture its daily optimal functioning. During these times, it becomes even more important to fol-low the **ON** Plan, eat small frequent meals, and focus on starch.

Sleep appears to be more important for the brain than it is for the body. When you don't get enough sleep, your sleep-deprived brain cells sleep through the alarm clock as they are still in the midst of a pleasant dream, have a difficult time co-ordinating motor function as you fall out of bed, and may take an hour to become fully alert and functioning. So what do you do? Gulp down some caffeine and sugar to jump-start your brain and give you a false sense of wakefulness that doesn't last long. Within an hour, your brain will be requesting a nap.

•

Speaking of naps, they can be restorative when you are sleep-deprived unless you nap more than ninety minutes. Long naps interfere with sleep that night and will result in sleep deprivation the next day.

You cannot live without sleep, but no one has ever died from sleep deprivation. Your body won't let you. Of all the basic needs in life, sleep is most important. You could die from food deprivation, water deprivation, oxygen deprivation—but before you could possibly die from sleep deprivation, your body would give in to the need.

How many hours of sleep do you need a night? How many days a week do you get those required sleep hours?

Some of us are short sleepers requiring less than six hours of sleep a night, and others are long sleepers requiring more than eight hours of sleep a night. Some of us are morning people, rising early and going to bed early; others are evening people, rising late and staying up late. The type of person you are, and the number of hours you need depends on your personal biological clock.

One of the best things you can do to take care of yourself is to get a good night's sleep. The next day, your rhythms will be more in synch, your food cravings more manageable.

If you would like to get a good night's sleep, but can't because of insomnia, night sweats, or frequent nighttime awakenings, the **ON** plan will help. It will balance your brain chemicals during the day, so that your rhythms will naturally induce sleep at night. Healthy eating for a good night's sleep is your optimal eating routine: fueling your body during the day and feeding it little at night, balancing serotonin during the day so it aids sleep at night.

In addition, some people find that various remedies help them fall asleep more quickly:

•

- a warm glass of milk before bed; calcium is thought to be a relaxing mineral
- a few crackers or a piece of bread with some jam; some additional serotonin might help
- herbal tea with honey; there's an old Chinese proverb "honey sweetens the sleep"
- a long, hot bath half an hour before bedtime
- progressive relaxation; it helps you fall asleep more quickly

Whatever the cause of brain strain: sleep deprivation or chronic stress, the **ON** Plan can work to your advantage by helping to get your body back on track.

Those cultures famous for their longevity and great numbers of centurians (people who live to be one hundred-plus years old) have been studied for their "fountain of youth" secrets. One commonality of these cultures is that they have a daily routine from which they seldom deviate. They wake up at the same time of the day, they always eat a good-size breakfast and lunch, they never skip meals, they are active at the same times every day, and they go to sleep when they get tired. Their lifestyles are not devoid of fat, sugar, chocolate, and alcohol—but their lifestyles are devoid of binging. They don't do anything too much or too little.

Their routine is predictable and directed by their biological schedule, not by occupational schedules or daily planners. I will not promise that you will live to be one hundred years old, but I will promise that the **ON** Plan will get you on an eating routine that matches your rhythms and is optimal for longevity and general health.

Now that you have all the knowledge and skills to Follow Your Optimal Eating Routine every day, let's evaluate your progress over the last five weeks.

•

WEEK 5: YOUR <u>ON</u> PLAN EVALUATION

What has the <u>ON</u> Plan done for you? Have you turned on your female appetite, your female food cravings, your positive moods, and your well-being?

I do not expect that you have mastered the <u>ON</u> Plan in five weeks. I do, however, hope that you have begun fulfilling your food cravings and noticing the benefits. I hope that you have begun to permit your female food intuition to guide you to your optimal eating routine, and have used that intuition daily, monthly, and when your natural rhythms have been disrupted.

Back in Chapter 3, you filled out some questionnaires on each of the steps to assess your pre-<u>ON</u> Plan attitudes and habits. On the following pages are the same questionnaires to complete again. Without looking back (no cheating, please) rate the statements and then go back to Chapter 3 to compare your scores from five weeks ago.

•

STEP 1: TRUST YOUR FEMALE FOOD CRAVINGS

Rate the following statements as follows:
0—never
1—seldom
2—frequently
3—always

1. I try to deny my food cravings. _____

2. I diet to lose weight. _____

3. Once I start eating, I have a difficult time stopping. _____

4. If I fulfill my food cravings, I fear weight gain. _____

5. If I fulfill my food cravings, I fear that I'll have an unhealthy diet. _____

6. I label foods as "good" or "bad." _____

7. I feel guilty after eating the foods I crave. _____

8. I eat my pleasure foods when no one is around. _____

9. I feel that I lack willpower and discipline. _____

10. I eat for emotional reasons. _____

TOTAL _____

•

STEP 2: DISCOVER YOUR FEMALE PLEASURE FOODS

Rate each of the statements as follows:
0—never
1—seldom
2—frequently
3—always

1. I restrict chocolate in my diet. _____

2. I restrict sugar in my diet. _____

3. I restrict starch in my diet. _____

4. I restrict fat in my diet. _____

5. I restrict salt in my diet. _____

6. I feel that carbohydrates are fattening. _____

7. I try to find "healthier" substitutes for my food cravings. _____

8. I use sugar for a quick pick-me-up. _____

9. I try to follow a very low-sugar diet. _____

10. I try to follow a very low-fat diet. _____

TOTAL _____

•

STEP 3: LEARN HOW TO EAT FOR MAXIMUM SATISFACTION

Rate each of the statements as follows:
0—never
1—seldom
2—frequently
3—always

1. I eat quickly. _____

2. I barely chew my food. _____

3. I eat standing up. _____

4. I eat unconsciously. _____

5. I overeat the foods I crave. _____

6. I clean my plate. _____

7. My meals contain a protein source, starch, salad, and vegetable. _____

8. I use artificial sweeteners. _____

9. I buy "nonfat" foods. _____

10. I don't feel satisfied with food. _____

TOTAL _____

•

STEP 4: DISTRIBUTE YOUR FOOD TO MAXIMIZE MOOD

Rate each of the statements as follows:
0—never
1—seldom
2—frequently
3—always

1. I skip breakfast.   _____

2. I skip lunch.   _____

3. My biggest meal is dinner.   _____

4. My food cravings are strongest in the evening.   _____

5. I eat dinner after 7:00 P.M.   _____

6. I feel that snacking is "bad."   _____

7. I eat 3 times (or fewer) a day.   _____

8. I snack before going to bed.   _____

9. I drink more than 2 cups of regular coffee a day.   _____

10. I don't have time for a leisurely lunch.   _____

TOTAL   _____

•

STEP 5: FOLLOW YOUR OPTIMAL EATING ROUTINE

Rate each of the statements as follows:
0—never
1—seldom
2—frequently
3—always

1. I have daily mood swings. _____

2. I have overwhelming fatigue. _____

3. I experience the 3:30 P.M. slump. _____

4. I'm depressed during the winter months. _____

5. I have difficulty sleeping at night. _____

6. I experience PMS or menopausal tension. _____

7. I crave more foods during the winter
months. _____

8. I crave more foods during PMS or
menopause. _____

9. I eat more sugar and fat when I am
stressed. _____

10. I have difficulty controlling my weight. _____

TOTAL _____

•

	TODAY'S SCORES	PREVIOUS SCORES
Step 1: Trust Your Female Food Cravings	_____	_____
Step 2: Discover Your Female Pleasure Foods	_____	_____
Step 3: Learn How to Eat for Maximum Satisfaction	_____	_____
Step 4: Distribute Your Food to Maximize Mood	_____	_____
Step 5: Practice Your Optimal Eating Routine	_____	_____
TOTAL SCORE	_____	_____
TOTAL CHANGE	_____	

In which steps did you experience the most change? Which will require some additional attention in the weeks ahead?

It doesn't matter how much you changed. What matters is that you are moving in the right direction. The goal is not to reduce every score to zero; there is no perfect score in the **ON** Plan!

The goal is to continue with the **ON** Plan for the next five weeks and the rest of your life. Continue keeping the eating records from Step 4 for as long as you find them helpful—and read the last two chapters. They will put on the finishing touches with exercise and empowerment!

•

Nine

THE <u>ON</u> EXERCISE PLAN:

YOUR FORMULA FOR

FEMALE FITNESS

I F YOU WERE INFORMED OF THE LATEST medical breakthrough for women that would significantly
temper sugar and fat cravings, reduce depression, manage stress, minimize symptoms of PMS and menopausal tension, mitigate sleep difficulties, stabilize mood, and guarantee
permanent weight loss without pills, negative side effects, or a
lighter wallet—would you seek out the miracle cure? Well,
you don't have to look far to find it. That medical breakthrough is exercise.

You are three-quarters of the way through the book and
were perhaps hoping that exercise would not be specifically
addressed or strongly encouraged. I've briefly mentioned the
endorphin-releasing effects of exercise a couple of times in
the previous chapters, but exercise is so important to a
woman's mood, mind, and body that it definitely warrants its
own chapter—not just a chapter that provides generic information on exercise, but a chapter that recognizes the special
exercise needs of all women.

•

Women have a unique physiology, stubborn fat cells, and an advanced brain chemistry; therefore, we need an exercise program designed specifically for us. We need an *optimal exercise routine* that will complement our *optimal eating routine*—and that optimal exercise routine is the <u>ON</u> Exercise Plan. It will turn on your positive moods, your productive energy, your female metabolism, and your healthy weight.

Like many of my clients, you may have "tried" exercise a number of times in the past and concluded that it simply doesn't work for you. Each time Marypat attempted an exercise program, she gained weight, felt more fatigued, and noticed stronger food cravings. She used to label herself "the first female to flunk exercise 101" until she started following the <u>ON</u> Exercise Plan and felt her spirits lift, her cravings diminish, and her weight drop.

If you have tried exercise and failed—**you didn't fail the exercise program, the exercise program failed you** because the guidelines weren't right for your female physiology. The program wasn't a formula for female fitness. Most of the exercise research has either focused on how to enhance the physical performance of competitive athletes or on how to reduce the heart disease risk of men, but little has been done on how it benefits women's physical and mental well-being.

Or maybe the exercise program you tried didn't work because it was too much like a diet. If your commitment to exercise started with an announcement like this, "I'm going on a weight-reducing exercise plan starting Monday, and I'm going to do it every day so that I will lose weight quickly and drop ten pounds in one month," you were doomed from the start. Physiologically, your female body is not going to respond well to an overzealous exercise program.

Within the first few days of a strenuous exercise regime, your female fat cells start fighting against your efforts. "Hey, what's going on here? She's trying to burn hundreds of calo-

•

ries every day at that gym down the street. I might be willing to give up a little of this precious gold mine of stored fat, but she's trying to force it out of me. Sorry, no can do. I might need my fat for an emergency. What if she gets pregnant to-night *and* a famine hits tomorrow? Close the door, lock the windows; I'm keeping my fat stores hostage no matter how much she exercises."

Overexercise causes a starvation response similar to that of dieting. The red warning lights flash an emergency warning, fat cells go into hibernation, metabolism slows down, and the signals are sent to use sugar and muscle for energy instead of fat. There is a new term to describe people who overexercise, hypergymnasiacs. I have counseled at least a hundred who have been exercising two hours every day for months, but have seen little, if any, change in their bodies, and therefore think they are a failure even at exercise. They expect me to tell them to exercise longer, harder, and more frequently. Instead, I tell them to exercise less, and they are shocked by the advice. By exercising more moderately, they will turn off the starvation response and turn on their fat-releasing, mood-enhancing exercise response.

The good news is that women are starting to replace diet plans with exercise programs. Instead of going on a liquid fast, women are going to a fitness facility. The disappointing news is that many still have the "quick weight loss" mentality and are going overboard on exercise.

It's no different from dieting. The more calories you try to burn and the quicker you try to lose the weight, the more your fat cells will fight back and the less weight you will lose.

If your exercise program isn't working for you, you are either exercising too much or, the other possibility, not enough. Either extreme is not going to give you the benefits. Just as there is a middle ground with food, there is a middle

•

ground with exercise—not every day and not once a month. You've found your optimal eating routine with the **ON** Plan, now it's time to find your optimal exercise routine. Exercise works for every woman as long as she is following the right guidelines for the female body—and realistically integrating them into her life.

There are two overall goals of your optimal exercise routine.

1. to stimulate mood-enhancing chemicals in your brain cells
2. to stimulate fat loss from your fat cells

With the **ON** Exercise Plan for Female Fitness you will simultaneously achieve both of these goals, and thus will receive all of the amazing benefits of exercise.

By stimulating brain chemical release, you will:

- improve mood
- temper sugar and fat cravings
- crave a wider variety of foods, including more vegetables and starch
- reduce PMS and perimenopausal tension and the food cravings during these times
- cope with stress and reduce stress-induced food cravings
- increase energy and productivity
- improve sleep quality

By stimulating fat loss, you will:

- achieve a comfortable, realistic weight
- reduce body fat
- boost metabolism

•

- contour your body shape
- reduce your risk of the weight-related diseases: heart disease, cancer, and diabetes

If you are going to spend precious time exercising, I want you to get all of these wonderful benefits. Let's first address the exercise-mood benefits.

EXERCISE, ENDORPHINS, AND LSD

You may have heard that exercise releases the mood-elevating endorphins, but what kind of exercise? How much? The answer is LSD. Not the LSD drug (although I hope it got your attention), but LSD exercise:

<u>L</u>ong
<u>S</u>low
<u>D</u>istance

Long, slow distance encourages the endorphin release because it uses the right muscles, the right nerves, and puts the right type of pain on the body for the right length of time. Endorphins are the body's natural painkillers and are released during long, painful experiences. You may personally think exercise is a "pain in the butt," but it produces the perfect type of long-term physical pain to make your brain want to release endorphins to help dull that pain.

As an interesting aside, if it weren't for women, perhaps natural painkilling endorphins wouldn't exist at all. Some anthropologists believe that women were the first gender to manufacture these natural opiates. Childbirth is a wonderful experience, but it is also a painful one. During childbirth, endorphins are released at about 200 times their normal levels

•

to withstand the hours (for some women many, many hours) of pain. Thousands of years ago there were no epidurals or drugs, and Mother Nature was looking out for our welfare with the release of endorphins during childbirth. You may argue that Mother Nature could have done a better job because childbirth is still painful, but imagine what it would be like without endorphins.

Back to exercise. Exercise creates a physical pain in your muscles, joints, and cardiovascular system, but it is a beneficial pain because your body gradually becomes stronger. While you are out for your walk or bike ride, endorphins are released as an analgesic. That analgesic works best with the long, dull pain produced from long, slow exercise.

How much LSD exercise do you need to stimulate an endorphin release? More than the standard exercise recommendation of twenty minutes, three times a week.

If you are out for your twenty-minute power walk, you may feel better, less stressed, and more energetic—and attribute those positive changes to the endorphins, but the exercise duration was not long enough to stimulate the need for an endorphin release. Most likely, you feel better because you got away from the rat race, spent some time alone, and released some pent-up energy.

With only twenty minutes of exercise, your brain thinks you can cope with the pain just fine on your own. But if you continue your power walk for another twenty minutes or so, your brain will start to feel sorry for you and will give you a helping hand by releasing endorphins. Do it long, do it slow, and go the distance for at least **forty-five minutes, three times a week.**

How can you tell if you are releasing endorphins with exercise?

If you are asking this question, then you probably haven't

•

experienced them. An identifiable altered state of consciousness is created, and some people even claim visions and hallucinations. I once had a client who claimed she saw pink flying elephants while exercising. I always wondered if exercise was the only drug she was on, but endorphins are a powerful morphinelike drug, so you never know.

You can feel confident that you are releasing endorphins when:

- All of a sudden, you get renewed physical energy and feel like you could keep exercising for hours.
- You have a floating sensation where your feet feel like they are barely touching the ground.
- Your senses become easily stimulated; colors look brighter, and your eyes and ears have heightened awareness.
- You have creative thoughts, inspiring ideas, and ingenious solutions to problems.

And, perhaps most important, you notice significant changes in your mood, energy level, productivity, and food cravings after you exercise.

From my research survey, those women who exercised regularly had fewer cravings because the exercise-induced endorphin release was substituting for the food-induced endorphin release. Compared to sedentary women, the regular exercisers reported:

- 39% fewer fat cravings
- 32% fewer chocolate cravings
- 22% fewer sugar cravings

Exercise stabilizes blood sugar levels and initiates the same brain chemical changes as high-sugar/high-fat foods.

●

When the brain's baseline endorphin level is increased with regular LSD exercise, there is no longer the need to send as frequent and as strong food craving signals. **Maybe there is a satisfying substitute for chocolate—exercise!**

This explains the well-documented observation that a regular exercise program naturally leads to positive changes in eating habits. When people start taking care of their bodies through an exercise program, they begin taking care of themselves in other ways. They feel so good from the endorphin release and other benefits of exercise, that they want to respond to their body's food needs. From my survey, I found that women who exercise regularly are:

- 50% more likely to eat 5 small meals a day
- 34% more likely to crave vegetables
- 50% less likely to use artificial fats and sweeteners
- 32% less likely to binge on their craved foods

In other words, regular exercisers automatically start following the steps of the **ON** Plan, and the combination of an optimal exercise routine with an optimal nutrition routine turns on their positive moods and energy. Regular exercisers are:

- 54% less likely to report daily fatigue
- 49% less likely to report depression
- 37% less likely to report mood swings
- 20% less likely to report sleep difficulties
- 20% less likely to report stress eating

With all of the research that I have compiled and analyzed on the mood-altering benefits from exercise, a story that my brother-in-law tells (over and over again) suddenly makes a

•

world of sense. The story is about a man who was stressed, depressed, overweight, had insomnia, was drinking too much, and was failing at work and at home, so he decided to commit suicide by running himself to death. That afternoon, he ran as far as he could, but to his disappointment, he didn't die. So the next day he tried to commit suicide by running again, but it still didn't work. He tried every day for six weeks and suddenly felt so good that he decided to live.

Making a commitment to the **ON** Exercise Plan will make you feel terrific and live life to its fullest. However, if your cravings are strong and your brain has been under considerable strain because of premenstrual tension, the winter blues, stress, or sleep deprivation—the timing of your workouts may be helpful to get your body's routine back on track.

If your difficult craving time is in the afternoon (which is the case for most women), then schedule your exercise for the hours of 11:00 A.M. to 3:00 P.M. This routine will help by boosting your brain chemicals when you need them the most and reducing the need for food to stabilize mood in the afternoon.

If your difficult craving time is in the evening, then scheduling exercise between the hours of 3:00 P.M. and 7:00 P.M. will help for the same reasons. Late-afternoon exercise also appears to be the best for a good night's sleep.

"I feel like my difficult eating time is all day long. Should I schedule exercise morning, noon, and night?" If you can't identify a specific time of day that exercise will be most beneficial, then do it any time it fits into your schedule. If there is no conceivable time that exercise will fit into your schedule, then you have to reevaluate your priorities. You must have the perseverance to somehow, some way make the time. Exercise is too important not to do it.

If you can't precisely time your workouts to tame your

•

cravings because of work and/or family commitments, have no fear. In the long run, any time of the day you work out is beneficial. It will increase your baseline of endorphins, increase your cravings for starches and vegetables, and curb your cravings for high-fat/high-sugar foods. **What's most important is that you exercise for forty-five minutes three times a week.** If you have the time to work out four or five times a week, please do! Just don't do it every day; your brain, muscles, joints, and heart need rest too. Rest is a part of taking care of yourself.

Remember: Long, slow distance will release endorphins, curb cravings, and elevate mood because it produces the right type of pain on the body. Even though I don't particularly care for the exercise slogan "no pain, no gain," it holds true as long as you are not exercising too hard and producing too much pain. For women, if it's too hard or too painful, that slogan becomes "no pain, no gain—and no weight loss either."

THE FEMALE FITNESS FORMULA FOR FAT-BURNING

So far in this book, you have learned how to work with your female appetite and your female food cravings to achieve the optimal nutrition solution for mind and body. In this chapter, you have learned how to work with your female brain and body to achieve the optimal exercise solution for mental health. Now for some advice on how to work with your female fat cells to achieve the optimal exercise solution for permanent weight loss.

Although I wish that health were the primary exercise motivator for most women, it isn't; weight loss and appearance are. So let's use these motivators. Exercise is the most

•

effective strategy to lose weight, contour our bodies, get rid of the saddlebags and love handles, and improve our self-image.

If you are going to spend the time exercising, I want you to receive all of the benefits that are important to you. The LSD approach to exercise will help you to accomplish it all: weight loss, mental health, and physical health. If you run as fast as you can for twenty minutes, that's not LSD exercise. You won't release many endorphins in your brain, and you won't release much fat from your fat cells.

Instead, if you walk for forty-five minutes at a slower pace, you'll stimulate maximum release of endorphins in your brain and maximum release of fat from your fat cells.

As we discussed at the beginning of this chapter, too much exercise can work against your female physiology, and whenever your fat cells feel threatened, they will fight back. You have to ease them slowly into exercise so that they almost don't realize what is going on.

When you first start walking (or cycling or swimming), your stubborn fat cells say, "Excuse me. What do you think you're doing? I detect some aerobic exercise going on here, and I know exactly what you want me to do. Sorry—I was born to store fat, not release it, and I'm not giving in." Then as you continue with your nonthreatening long, slow distance, your fat cells finally give in. "Well, all right. You've been doing this for thirty minutes now and it's not too strenuous or too threatening. I'll give up some fat, but not a lot and not for too long."

Long, slow, distance is the secret to endorphin release and fat release for women. As a matter of fact, LSD exercise is the *only* way to stimulate the release of fat. There is no food, drink, cream, pill, potion, salve, gadget, or device that will

•

shrink your fat cells. Only long, slow exercise with the Female Fitness Formula will do it. Maybe you were expecting something a little more exciting like, "Eat chocolate and shrink your fat cells forever." Sorry, even though it sensibly goes along with this book title and chocolate does do wonders for your female mind—it doesn't help you burn fat. The secret is exercise, and there are special fat-burning guidelines for women.

FAT-BURNING EXERCISE GUIDELINES FOR WOMEN

1. **Choose an aerobic exercise, any aerobic exercise**   Aerobic means "with oxygen" and a sufficient supply of oxygen is necessary to stimulate the fat-releasing enzymes while exercising. Aerobic exercise uses your major muscle groups (the buttocks and thighs) in a rhythmical, nonstop fashion and increases your rate of breathing and the delivery of oxygen (O_2 = oxygen) to your fat cells.

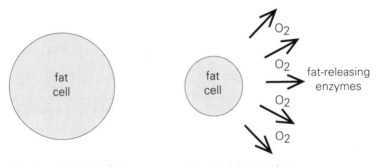

without aerobic exercise   with aerobic exercise

Whether it's walking, jogging, biking, swimming, rowing, cross country skiing, jumping rope, or going to aerobic classes, all aerobic exercises are created equal and will stim-

•

ulate the fat-releasing enzymes. Anaerobic (without oxygen) exercises such as tennis, softball, weight lifting, and golf are stop/start movements and do not keep your rate of breathing consistently high. However, they still tone your muscles and boost your metabolism, so if you enjoy them, please don't stop; just add an aerobic exercise.

2. **Do it at a moderate intensity and never, ever get out of breath** Because a sufficient oxygen supply is necessary to stimulate the fat-releasing enzymes and burn fat, your rate of breathing and the delivery of oxygen are extremely important. Your rate of breathing has to be increased, but if you are huffing and puffing, the exercise is too hard and the oxygen demands cannot be met through respiration. The result: Your fat cells feel threatened, and your body uses sugar and muscle for energy instead of fat.

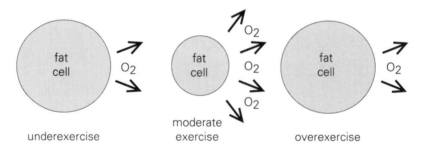

How can you tell if you are exercising moderately? I will share two methods with you: the target heart rate method and the sing test. Because the sing test is usually the most accurate (and my favorite), let's start with that one first.

That's right, I am going to ask you to sing while you are exercising. You don't have to sing the opera *La Bohème* or the national anthem (unless you want to); you can sing any-

•

thing from a nursery rhyme to your favorite song. You also don't have to sing during your entire workout; I want you to check in every five minutes or so with just one or two lines.

The sing test works like this:

- If you can easily sing with no need to take a breath at all, then you are not exercising hard enough.
- If you have to take a breath between every syllable, then you are exercising too hard.
- If you take a couple of breaths evenly dispersed, then you are exercising just right and it's moderate.

The target heart rate method uses an equation that estimates your maximum heart rate and takes percentages to determine a moderate range.

(220 − your age) × 60% = your lower target heart rate
(220 − your age) × 75% = your upper target heart rate

For example, if you are forty years old:

220 − 40 = 180 × 60% = 108 beats per minute
220 − 40 = 180 × 75% = 135 beats per minute
Target Heart Rate Range is 108 to 135 beats per minute

With this method, you have to find your pulse, count the seconds, and count the beats at the same time. Some people have a tough time finding their pulse (and wonder if they are still alive), while others find it difficult to count the seconds and count the beats because they lose count. Unless you are a seasoned pulse taker, I encourage you to use the sing test and monitor your rate of breathing. Who

•

knows, you may even have more fun exercising if you sing your way through it!

3. **Do it a minimum of forty-five minutes** The stubborn female fat cell needs some coaxing and some time to test the waters and slowly release fat. For the first thirty minutes of exercise, your fat cells are activating the fat-burning enzymes and getting ready to release fat, but they won't give in to your efforts until they are absolutely sure that it's necessary and it's safe. With a very moderate intensity, they will not feel threatened, but it still takes about thirty minutes before they start to significantly give up fat. However, once the fat-releasing enzymes are activated, you have entered the fat-burning zone and every minute after thirty minutes is a guaranteed fat-burning minute.

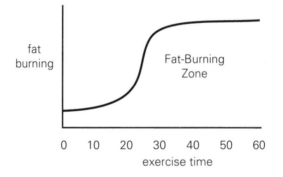

The first half hour is not useless exercise; you are stimulating your metabolism and burning calories, but those calories are primarily coming from sugar stores, not fat stores. If you exercise for the full forty-five minutes, then you have at least fifteen minutes of pure fat-burning exercise.

"Why does my husband run for twenty minutes three times a week and immediately lose weight? Do men release fat sooner?" asked a perplexed Victoria. While it takes

•

most of us a half hour to start releasing fat, men will release fat within minutes of exercising. It may not seem fair, but it's a medical fact. While we are born with the fat-storing machinery to gain weight quickly and efficiently, men are born with the fat-burning machinery to lose weight quickly and efficiently. They don't have a lot of estrogen and the special functions of pregnancy and breast-feeding.

Equality of the sexes doesn't extend to fat-burning and weight loss. Then again, equality of the sexes doesn't extend to the food-mood connection either. Men may lose fat more quickly, but they are also less likely to benefit from the mood-enhancing qualities of chocolate. We *can* make our bodies burn fat by exercising longer, but men probably *can't* make their brains happy even if they eat a pound of chocolate.

4. **Do it a minimum of three times a week**   To see a significant, permanent change in your body, you need to exercise moderately for forty-five minutes, three times a week. Exercising once or twice a week isn't enough to keep your body conditioned to release fat. If you want to exercise four or five times a week, you'll notice changes a little more quickly, but three times a week is all you need.

5. **Stimulate your muscle mass to boost your metabolism** The aerobic activity itself will stimulate your muscles in the buttocks and thighs, but to boost your metabolism and fat-burning capacity even more, you may want to consider a light weight-training program. Consult an exercise physiologist who can design a program that's right for you.

These are the five fat-burning exercise guidelines for women. Whatever aerobic activity you choose, make sure that it follows *all* of the guidelines. If it does, then you will

•

transform your fat-storing body into a fat-burning body. Walking is as good as biking, which is as good as swimming, which is as good as rowing, and so on.

Chrisi asked with some embarrassment, "Is sex considered a good fat-burning aerobic exercise?" Well, if it is rhythmical, nonstop movement using your buttocks and thighs at a moderate intensity for at least forty-five minutes three times a week, then it fits the fat-burning criteria. Her quick response was, "Never mind. How about square dancing?"

OVERCOMING EXERCISE ANXIETY

"Just hearing that I don't have to do it any more than three times a week releases the anxiety for me. I never started exercising because I always thought that I would have to do it six or seven days a week for the rest of my life." Most women are quite pleased with the three days a week recommendation, although some are not as happy with the forty-five-minute duration. But if you want the mood-enhancing, fat-burning benefits, forty-five minutes is necessary. As a matter of fact, you will experience more benefit exercising three times a week for forty-five minutes than you would five times a week for thirty minutes—and that's fifteen minutes less exercise time a week!

You now know how to exercise for the simultaneous release of both the endorphins in your brain and the fat from your female fat cells. But knowledge does not always translate into action. You know you should be doing it, you know how to do it with the Female Fitness Formula, but exercise anxiety can prevent you from making the lifelong commitment to do it.

Exercise anxiety comes from a number of different

•

sources. Here are some common sources of anxiety that you may be experiencing.

1. **"Once I start exercising, I'll have to do it for the rest of my life."** My hope is that once you start, the emotional and physical benefits will be so great that you will want to do it for the rest of your life. As you begin exercising, don't force yourself to make a firm commitment for the next thirty or forty years. Take the "one week at a time" approach. Each week make a commitment to the days you will do it and the number of minutes you will do it.

2. **"I don't have an extra forty-five minutes in my day to exercise."** This is a big one. We are so busy taking care of everyone else and everything else, that we don't have the time to take care of ourselves through exercise, eating, or any other means. Analyze your weekly schedule: Exactly where can you envision exercise fitting into that schedule? If your immediate answer is "never"—keep looking long and hard. Can you do it Saturday and Sunday, then just one other day during the week?

3. **"I don't like to exercise and won't be able to find something that I will enjoy."** To stick with it, you have to at least find it acceptable. If you know that you don't like to swim, don't choose swimming. If you find the stationary bike boring, don't invest in one. Today there are so many exercise options to choose from: gyms, aerobics studios, walking groups, walking paths, swimming teams, hiking clubs, well-designed home exercise equipment. Do some experimentation. If you don't like what you've chosen, try something else. I won't guarantee that you will grow to love exercise, but it will become such an integral part of your quality of life that without it you won't feel like yourself. You will look forward to the endorphin release!

•

Because of the sometimes paralyzing exercise anxiety, I have adopted the one-small-step-at-a-time approach to exercise—*to slowly build your exercise program over a period of three months.*

Can you do it one day over the next week? Most women say sure. Can you add a few more minutes? Can you add one more day? Slowly add the number of minutes per session and the number of days until you have built up to three forty-five-minute sessions a week. This slow approach will not only help you make exercise a permanent part of your life, but will also reduce the chances of initial injury. In addition, I recommend consulting your physician before starting any exercise program. The final section of this chapter will help you to use this slow, easy approach and design your own **ON** Exercise Plan.

THE WOMAN'S WORKOUT: DESIGNING YOUR PROGRAM

If exercise is already a part of your life, Congratulations! Continue with what you are doing and revise it if necessary to match the Female Fitness Formula for endorphin and fat release. If you are just beginning, then take it slowly and design an exercise program that will keep you fit by fitting into your lifestyle.

Although you will notice the psychological benefits of increased energy and productivity a lot sooner, I suggest making a three month commitment to condition your fat cells to release fat. At the end of three months, your body fat will be significantly lower and your moods and energy significantly higher.

First, what aerobic activity will you choose? If you are not sure, I suggest starting with walking. It's inexpensive and you

•

can do it anywhere. You can also choose a variety of activities; walk one day, swim another day, and go to an aerobics class the last day.

Once you've chosen your activity, then choose the days of the week that you'll do it and slowly build your exercise program over the next twelve weeks to achieve LSD exercise without anxiety or potential injury.

Weeks 1 & 2:	exercise 1 session a week for 10 to 15 minutes
Weeks 3 & 4:	exercise 2 sessions a week for 20 minutes
Weeks 5 & 6:	exercise 3 sessions a week for 30 minutes
Weeks 7 & 8:	exercise 3 sessions a week for 35 minutes
Weeks 9 & 10:	exercise 3 sessions a week for 40 minutes
Weeks 11 & 12:	exercise 3 sessions a week for 45 minutes

Remember: The type of exercise you choose doesn't matter as long as it is aerobic, you enjoy it, and you never get out of breath.

Like the eating records in the **ON** Plan, exercise records can also help you to monitor your progress and watch your exercise program grow to its full potential. For each week, under the days that you exercised, record the number of minutes that you were exercising in your moderate fat-burning zone. There is an example and a blank record on the following pages.

You *can* successfully make exercise a part of your life by following a workout designed specifically for your female physiology, progressively building your program, and realistically scheduling it into your life. Good luck!

•

THE **ON** PLAN EXERCISE RECORD

	Mon	Tues	Wed	Thurs	Fri	Sat	Sun
Week 1			15 min				
Week 2					15 min		
Week 3			20 min		20 min		
Week 4			20 min		20 min		
Week 5	30 min		30 min		30 min		
Week 6		30 min	30 min		30 min		
Week 7	35 min		35 min		35 min		
Week 8		35 min			35 min	35 min	
Week 9			40 min		40 min	40 min	
Week 10	40 min		40 min		40 min		
Week 11	45 min		45 min				45 min
Week 12	45 min		45 min		45 min		

THE **ON** PLAN EXERCISE RECORD

	Mon	Tues	Wed	Thurs	Fri	Sat	Sun
Week 1							
Week 2							
Week 3							
Week 4							
Week 5							
Week 6							
Week 7							
Week 8							
Week 9							
Week 10							
Week 11							
Week 12							

●

Ten

EMPOWERMENT EATING FOR A

LIFETIME OF WELL-BEING

I APPRECIATE MY FOOD CRAVINGS for the special purpose they serve. I have reconnected my food-mood link and have lost weight. I am feeding and exercising my body with specific guidelines designed for a woman's body. And the best part is that I finally understand the way my female body functions. I feel so empowered!"

Knowledge and understanding are empowering. If you understand the way your female body functions, you'll know what makes sense and what's right for you—and you'll be empowered to continue treating your body with health, kindness, and respect.

E ating + E xercise = E mpowerment

•

I want you to take all that positive energy, trust, under-standing, knowledge, skill, accomplishment, and empower-ment—and use it to fulfill all of your female needs today, to-morrow, and for the rest of your life.

FEEL GOOD TODAY, STAY HEALTHY TOMORROW

Isn't that the ultimate well-being goal—feel good today and reduce your risk of disability and disease tomorrow? The two parts of the goal are not mutually exclusive—you can fulfill your immediate daily needs and your long-term health needs simultaneously.

Your short-term and long-term health goals are no differ-ent from any other goals in your life. You want to pick up the dry cleaning today *and* reorganize your closet over the next month. You want to get your kids to preschool today *and* pre-pare for their college education fifteen years from now. We often accomplish today's "to do" list, but procrastinate with tomorrow's goals. It's the same with health goals.

The truth is, most people are not motivated by the long-term health benefits of exercising or changing their eating habits. Instead, they are motivated by what they will immedi-ately get out of positive lifestyle changes. It's human nature to be impatient and want quick results.

As a health professional, I'm the first to admit that we haven't done a very good job of motivating people to prevent heart disease, stroke, cancer, and diabetes. The incidence of these diseases continues to climb each year. We have, how-ever, been quite successful in motivating people to make posi-tive lifestyle changes once they are diagnosed with a disease. Mortality rates for cardiovascular diseases and cancers have

•

decreased each year, but my profession doesn't deserve much credit. These people (you may be one of them) are highly motivated to prevent death and seek out the proper treatment.

I can't begin to count the number of times I have heard my clients say something like this. "I'm feeling fine and I'm disease-free, so why should I reduce my fat intake? My chances of getting hit by a car tomorrow are greater than my chances of dying from heart disease twenty years from now." I can't argue with statistics or human nature, so I have changed my approach.

In the past, I have used the thoughtful phrase:

"An ounce of prevention equals a pound of cure."

But, thoughtful or not, you may not care about curing anything right now except perhaps a sick child. You may, however, care quite a bit about feeling happiness in the midst of unhappy life events. So, now I have added an additional thought-provoking phrase:

"An ounce of prevention equals a pound of cure."
and . . .
"An ounce of chocolate equals a pound of happiness."

Why can't you have both? Happiness today and reduced risk of disease tomorrow. Chocolate today and prevention tomorrow. **YOU CAN!!**

You can receive the immediate, motivating benefits of your optimal eating and exercise routine and simultaneously receive the long-term benefits, too. Actually, you already have received the immediate benefits of the **ON** Eating and Exercise Plan:

•

enhanced mood
reduced stress
increased energy
reduced PMS and menopausal tension
reduced weight

At the same time, you can also reduce your risk of the chronic lifestyle diseases in the future. If you have a family history of heart disease, if you are at risk for osteoporosis, or if you fear the rising epidemic of breast cancer—the **ON** Plan may help you to reduce your long-term risk of these diseases and promote longevity.

"You mean chocolate will reduce my risk of breast cancer?" Chocolate has many unique qualities, but it is not an anti-disease agent. A moderate amount, however, will not increase your risk of breast cancer or heart disease. As I have said many times and will reiterate once again—women require slightly more sugar and fat than men, and a moderate amount of chocolate or any other high-fat/high-sugar food will not be harmful. It's restriction and binge eating that are: not eating any chocolate, then eating pounds of chocolate.

By trusting and responding to your body's needs with the **ON** Plan, you have found that peaceful, realistic, attainable area of moderation that will give you the immediate *and* long-term benefits.

However, if you would like further dietary guidance on the three top women's health concerns—osteoporosis, breast cancer, and heart disease—read on. Additional knowledge and understanding will lead to further empowerment, and that additional empowerment will lead to a healthier body and mind.

•

BONING UP ON OSTEOPOROSIS

Osteoporosis is the premature loss of calcium from your bones. Some loss naturally occurs with age, but waiting until the menopausal years to be concerned is not in your best interest. Peak bone mass is reached in the early twenties, and women start to lose calcium from their bones at around age thirty (men not until age fifty or sixty). We then lose it at an accelerated rate when estrogen declines during menopause. If you are already in your menopausal years, it's never too late to use your optimal eating and exercise routine to prevent further bone loss.

How does the **ON** Plan fulfill your needs for bone health?

You may have been concerned that milk products and calcium sources were not a primary focus of the **ON** Plan. Your body and bones do need calcium daily, but osteoporosis has been erroneously viewed as a problem of calcium deficiency. Women have been popping calcium supplements and downing glasses of milk for over a decade now trying to "correct" their calcium deficiency—and overall bone mass hasn't significantly increased. There's more to the osteoporosis story than just calcium.

Osteoporosis is not so much a problem with calcium deficiency as it is a problem with negative calcium balance in the body—when more calcium is excreted through your kidneys and colon than is absorbed in your bloodstream and deposited in your bones. When this happens, the bones don't have the calcium available to become stronger.

This negative calcium balance can be caused by a number of dietary factors, but one of the major calcium robbers appears to be protein. When the by-product of protein is excreted through the kidneys, it grabs calcium and takes it along for the ride. The **ON** Plan has de-emphasized protein be-

•

cause it may interfere with the mood-enhancing benefits of carbohydrates, but protein also interferes with the bone-building benefits of calcium. An added benefit of listening to your body and eating less protein is that you will help put your body in a more positive calcium balance.

Of course women need some protein to repair muscle and manufacture enzymes, but the average woman consumes 1½ times the amount her body needs. That excess protein may be having a negative effect on mood and bone health. A moderate, female-friendly protein intake would be at least a three-ounce portion of a high quality animal or vegetable protein source a day. That, in combination with the protein in all the grains you are eating throughout the day, is enough to fulfill your needs.

Besides protein, there are other calcium robbers:

caffeine
sodium
soft drinks
alcohol

Caffeine and sodium work similarly to protein: When they are filtered through the kidneys, they rob the body and bones of a few molecules of calcium. Soft drinks (especially diet!) have another mineral, phosphorous, that competes with calcium for absorption in your stomach and intestine. And alcohol reduces the absorption of calcium in your stomach *and* increases the calcium excreted in your urine.

No wonder the typical woman is at risk for osteoporosis. Think of what she does every day: She eats too much protein because of the heavy meat focus in westernized meals; she eats too much sodium because she's so busy and relies on quick processed foods; she has a couple of cups of coffee a day, a few

•

soft drinks, and a couple of glasses of wine. Her body may not know that a positive calcium balance can exist.

Watch your intake of these calcium robbers and keep your intake to moderate amounts. One to two a day for each is moderate: one or two cups of coffee (you already know this from Chapter 7), one to two soft drinks, and even one to two high-salt foods.

"Are you telling me that I don't have to worry about my calcium intake?" No, you need calcium to put you in positive calcium balance, but I'm telling you that no matter how much calcium you consume, these robbers can throw your calcium off balance.

How much calcium do you need to consume a day? It depends on who you ask. The World Health Organization says 450 mg/day, the Recommended Dietary Allowances say 800 mg/day, and the National Institutes of Health says 1,000 for premenopausal women and 1,500 mg/day for post-menopausal women. To be on the safe side, you should strive for the higher amounts.

One thousand mg to 1,500 mg is not that difficult to achieve. Yogurt contains 450 mg of calcium per serving, milk 300 mg, and most cheeses 200 mg. Even mineral water can significantly add to your daily calcium intake—most mineral waters have a range of 50 mg to 100 mg per cup. So, the calcium in water plus a couple of servings of milk products (along with what's present in the other foods you are eating) is usually enough to meet the recommendation. However, if you are lactose intolerant, a strict vegetarian, or don't drink milk for some other reason, be knowledgeable of the other sources of calcium.

•

SOURCES OF CALCIUM

sardines (3 oz)	372 mg	collard greens (½ c)	179 mg
tofu (3 oz)	120 mg	rhubarb (½ c)	175 mg
shrimp (3 oz)	100 mg	beet greens (½ c)	100 mg
legumes (1 c)	100 mg	broccoli (½ c)	55 mg
almonds (¼ c)	90 mg	spinach (½ c)	84 mg
orange (1 med)	50 mg	molasses (1 T)	137 mg

Focus on food sources first, supplements second. The calcium naturally found in food is better absorbed than the calcium in supplements. If you do take calcium supplements, use them as they were designed to be used: to supplement the calcium in your diet, not to replace it. The recommended calcium supplements are calcium carbonate and calcium citrate for best absorption by your body.

No matter how much calcium you consume or how cognizant you are of the calcium robbers, if you don't exercise, your body has no means of depositing the calcium in your bones. Yet another reason to commit to the **ON** Exercise Plan!

Weight-bearing exercise has always been and will always be the best for strengthening the bones. That doesn't mean that you have to start pumping iron to prevent bone loss; it means that you have to do something that forces your bones to carry the weight of your body over a distance.

That's why walking is great! You are moving your entire body weight with each step. With the stationary bike and rowing machine, most of your body weight is being supported by the seat (and that's why your seat can become quite uncomfortable) and not your bones.

"I quit swimming because someone told me that it wasn't doing any good for my bones." If you quit swimming and started walking, then that was better for your bones. If you

•

quit swimming and did nothing, then start swimming again. With swimming, the water is supporting your weight and you are floating, but with each kick and stroke, you are moving pounds and pounds of water. Other weight-bearing exercises are better, but you'll still get some bone benefit in the water.

Any movement that forces your bones to carry weight is beneficial.

> walking
> running
> cross-country skiing
> dancing
> aerobic dance classes
> step classes
> golf (as long as you don't use the cart)
> bowling
> tennis
> racquetball and squash
> basketball and softball
> rollerskating and Rollerblading
> weight lifting

Weight-bearing exercises are not limited to organized activities and sports. Becoming a new mother is enough to deposit lots of calcium in the bones—carrying the developing child for nine months, then carrying around the infant and all the accessories that go along with a baby. Some other weight-bearing activities include lawn mowing, gardening, and much to my chagrin, house cleaning.

Exercising your bones is one of your best defenses against osteoporosis. However, there are many reasons why we exercise, so the weight-bearing exercises that are also aerobic are the best choices for bone health, mood-enhancement, weight loss, and heart disease and breast cancer prevention.

•

GETTING TO THE HEART OF BREAST CANCER

When asked to rate their health concerns, women repeatedly report:

#1-breast cancer
#2-other cancers
#3-AIDS
#4-heart disease

To the surprise of many, breast cancer is not the leading cause of death for women; it's heart disease. And breast cancer is not the leading cause of cancer deaths any longer; it's lung cancer. Needless to say, increased smoking habits are responsible for the recent rise in female lung cancers.

Until recently, few heart disease studies included women, and in those that did, we were greatly underrepresented. Women have not only been neglected as test subjects in research—but also as patients in the doctor's office. Studies have shown the many physicians take men's symptoms seriously, while they are more likely to dismiss our cardiovascular complaints as psychosomatic.

We may not have heart attacks as early in life as men do or may not have as many heart attacks, but when we have one, we are about twice as likely to die from it. Over 36 percent of all female deaths each year are due to heart disease—*that's ten times more than die from breast cancer each year.*

I am by no means belittling breast cancer; over 45,000 women die each year, and I think about the possibility of breast cancer each morning in the shower. I am trying to put it into perspective to encourage you to combat both heart disease and breast cancer together.

Breast cancer and heart disease share a number of risk fac-

•

tors such as family history, smoking, obesity, and certain lifestyle habits. Others, however, are very different:

Heart Disease	Breast Cancer
high blood cholesterol	starting your period before age 12
high blood pressure	having your first birth after age 30
high triglycerides	having no children

"What about fibrocystic breast disease? Isn't that a risk factor for breast cancer?" I explained to Jenna that, first of all, having painful breast lumps is not a disease, and, second, if it were a risk factor, 90 percent of all women would be at increased risk. There are five different classifications for fibrocystic breasts, and they are all usually lumped together (pardon the pun), so women think that any type may lead to breast cancer. But only one, called atypical hyperplasia, has been linked to breast cancer, and it's one of the least common.

Some of the risk factors for heart disease and breast cancer such as family history and race you cannot control, but you *can* control the dietary risk factors! The **ON** Plan has already addressed some them.

- Maintain a comfortable weight—if you are not quite there yet, you are on your way. The **ON** Plan will continue to help you until you've reached your goal.
- Eat a moderately low-fat diet—you already are because you are listening to your body's needs and eating fat-friendly. Let me address the fat-disease link more specifically.

The relationship between fat and heart disease is fairly cut-and-dry. Too much fat, particularly saturated fat from animal sources, increases the artery-clogging "bad" choles-

•

terol. With the **ON** plan, you are eating more starch and less animal protein, so your saturated fat intake has automatically come down.

How much is too much fat? When more than 30 percent of your daily calories are derived from fat, it can start to have a negative effect on your arteries.

The relationship between fat and breast cancer is confusing and equivocal. While some studies have shown a link, others have found no connection at all. The jury is still out and will probably be in deliberation for another five years or so. What do you do in the meantime? Be prudent and eat a moderate amount of fat.

A range of 20 to 30 percent of your total calories should be about right. With the **ON** Plan, I hope that your body has naturally balanced your fat intake at this moderate level, but here are two more important suggestions:

1. If you are craving fat, fulfill the craving with as *small* an amount as you possibly can. Remember: It doesn't take much to satisfy biological food cravings.
2. When you eat a high-fat food, *balance* your fat intake over the rest of the day with lower-fat foods. For example, if you ate chocolate for your afternoon snack because "the galanin made you do it," then choose all low-fat foods for dinner when your brain isn't requesting anything in particular.

The following chart on the fat content of foods will help you to identify the higher-fat foods and confidently balance your day with low-fat foods.

There is one important dietary recommendation to reduce the risk of heart disease and breast cancer that hasn't been addressed yet: Eat five a day! It doesn't mean eat five small meals a day (although it could stand for that too); it

•

| **LOW IN FAT** | **HIGH IN FAT** |
| **<20% CALORIES FROM FAT** | **>20% CALORIES FROM FAT** |

PRODUCE

fruits and vegetables, fruit and vegetable juices, dried fruit, pickles, sauerkraut	olives, avocado, coconut, creamed vegetables, vegetable oils

STARCHES

most breads and cereals, bagels, English muffins, pasta, noodles, rice, corn, barley, bulgur, oats, bran, potatoes, corn tortillas, rice cakes, pretzels, water crackers, air-popped popcorn, matzoh	muffins, biscuits, corn bread, waffles, pancakes, granola, croissants, pastries, donuts, flour tortillas, french fries, hash browns, snack chips, most snack crackers, oil-popped and microwaved popcorn, wheat germ

DAIRY PRODUCTS

nonfat milk, nonfat dry milk, 1% low-fat milk, buttermilk, nonfat & low-fat yogurt, nonfat & low-fat frozen yogurt, nonfat & low-fat cottage cheese, ice milk, sherbet	whole milk, 2% low-fat milk, cream, half & half, whipped cream, ice cream, nondairy creamer, most cheeses, sour cream, cream cheese, creamed cottage cheese, butter

•

| LOW IN FAT | HIGH IN FAT |
| **<20% CALORIES FROM FAT** | **>20% CALORIES FROM FAT** |

PROTEIN FOODS

| | |
| halibut, cod, haddock, sole, flounder, red snapper, tuna, tuna in water, butterfish, shrimp, squid, clams, oysters, mussels, scallops, crab, white meat of poultry without skin, ham, Canadian bacon, pork loin, veal, round steak, flank steak, venison, rabbit, buffalo, egg whites, legumes | salmon, swordfish, shark, trout, mackerel, anchovies, sardines, dark meat of poultry, white meat of poultry with skin, most beef, most pork, most lamb, bacon, sausage, hot dogs, cold cuts, organ meats, nuts, seeds, refried beans, peanut butter, tofu, duck, eggs |

MISCELLANEOUS

| | |
| broths, bouillon, most soups, spices, herbs, salsa, mustard, ketchup, horseradish, soy sauce, teriyaki sauce, vinegar, Worchestershire sauce, wine, fat-free salad dressings | creamed soups, salad dressing, mayonnaise, margarine, oils, lard, beef tallow |

SUGAR FOODS AND DESSERTS

| | |
| jam, jelly, apple butter, sugar, jelly beans, hard candies, licorice, lollipops, Popsicles, fruit bars, sorbet, fig bars, animal crackers, ginger snaps, angel food cake, marshmallows, gelatin | chocolate, candy bars, most cookies, most cakes, pies, fudge, granola bars, Tofutti, ice cream |

•

means eat at least five fruits and/or vegetables a day. Why? Because over 200 research studies have found the same results: As the intake of fruits and vegetables increases, the risk of heart disease and cancer decreases.

What's so special about produce? Fruits and vegetables are low in fat, high in fiber, high in nutrients—and especially high in antioxidants.

Vitamin C, beta-carotene (the water soluble form of vitamin A), and other vitamins and minerals are antioxidants—meaning, "against oxidation." All of your body's cells use oxygen for the metabolic processes, and one of the waste products of cellular oxidation is called free radicals. I'm not talking about the people from the 1960s roaming the streets of Berkeley (although some are still there); I'm referring to unstable molecules that produce havoc in your body. Their sole goal is to stabilize themselves by interacting with other cells in the body. They could interact with a breast cell, an arterial cell, or any other cell—and when they do, they cause a chain reaction of free radicals and cellular damage.

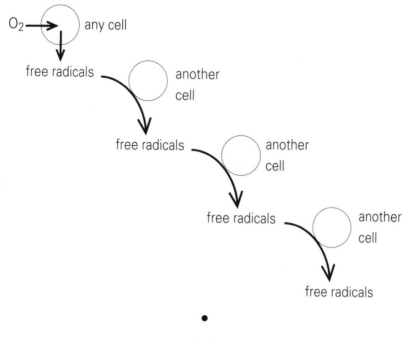

As the free radicals try to stabilize themselves, they cause injury to cells and trigger the formation of yet another free radical. You can't stop this process completely unless you stop breathing, and then you'll die anyway. However, you can slow down the oxidation process with antioxidants. They stabilize the free radicals without becoming injured or unstable themselves.

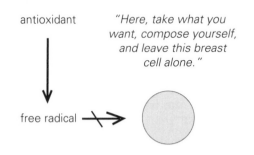

This is a simple explanation for a very complicated process, but I want you to understand why eating five fruits and vegetables a day is important.

Do you need more persuasion to focus on five a day? Fruits and vegetables also contain phytochemicals, powerful disease-fighting agents that may help to eliminate harmful substances from your body and reduce your risk of cancer. There are thousands of these phytochemicals in plants only (phyto means plant), and they have been called the new nutrients of the 90s.

How many do you eat a day? Only 23 percent of us eat five or more a day—and that's even an overestimate. In many of these food consumption surveys, ketchup is considered a fruit (tomatoes are really a fruit!) and french fries are considered a vegetable (potatoes are a vegetable even though we think of them mostly as a starch). **Make it a priority to eat five a day!**

•

When you are listening to your body's needs, five a day should come easy. You will crave vegetables for the nutrients your body needs. You will crave fruits for their nutrients too as well as for the sugar/serotonin release. To be sure that you are getting the antioxidants in your five a day, choose:

> 1 serving that's orange/yellow for a beta-carotene source: carrots, squash, cantaloupe, red bell peppers, papaya, apricots, tomatoes
> 1 serving that's citrus for a vitamin C source: oranges, grapefruit, strawberries, pineapple, nectarines
> 1 serving that's dark green for both the beta-carotene and vitamin C: broccoli, brussels sprouts, spinach, swiss chard, kale, romaine lettuce,
> 2 other servings of your choice
> (Note: 1 serving = ½ cup of cooked vegetables, ¾ cup of raw vegetables, or 1 medium fruit)

"Which category does chocolate fall into? It must be a vegetable because it comes from the cocoa plant." Michelle was really stretching it on that one. When she realized that chocolate did not qualify as a vegetable or fruit, her next question was, "Can I take supplements instead?"

If your body was designed to get its nutrients from supplements, then pills would grow on trees. Focus on food first and use supplements, if you need to, to give added insurance that you're getting what you need.

Many people take supplements for more than just assurance; they use them to replace food in their diets. They take their ten supplements each morning and think that they don't have to worry about healthy food choices all day long. Well, they still need to be concerned because vitamin supplements don't contain all the necessary vitamins. Prior to 1930, only eight essential nutrients had been discovered. In 1960, there

•

were about twenty-five—and today, there are over thirty-five essential nutrients that the body can't live without. The point that I'm trying to make is that supplement manufacturers can't predict the future; they can only rely on past research. The supplements you find in the health food store today are lacking in nutrients that haven't been discovered yet.

While we are on the topic of supplements, there are a number of vitamins, minerals, and other concoctions advertised to stabilize mood, boost energy, decrease stress, and reduce PMS and menopausal symptoms. Although some nutrients are needed in the conversion of carbohydrates to serotonin, taking the supplements is not the answer to mood control. There are many players in the food-mood connection—and real food provides them all.

BEYOND CHOCOLATE: OTHER MOOD ENHANCERS

You can exercise, eat chocolate, and fulfill your other female food needs to boost your mood and rejuvenate your body. In addition, I thought it would be helpful to briefly mention a few other activities that have been found to stimulate the release of endorphins and serotonin.

- water submersion, hydrotherapy, hot tubs, and hot baths
- acupressure, acupuncture, deep muscle massage, and shiatsu
- meditation, prayer, progressive relaxation, and biofeedback
- yoga and tai chi
- love, intimacy, and sexual pleasure
- even breast-feeding and mother-infant bonding have been found to trigger positive brain chemical changes in both the mother and the child

•

Many of these activities have been used for thousands of years in other countries, so their mind-body interactions are only new to us, but not to the world. Use them to complement the food-mood connection and your endorphin-releasing exercise program. They release the same pleasurable brain chemicals as eating chocolate, and perhaps more.

I once had a client who tried an at-home endorphin experiment with as many of these activities as she could. She went for a forty-five-minute walk, had a full-body massage, ate a piece of chocolate, meditated for an hour, went to a yoga class, ate another piece of chocolate, sat in the hot tub for twenty minutes, then made passionate love to her husband for an hour.

She reported such an altered state of consciousness that she "was in La-La Land for days and had the best week of her life." The only problem was that she was so relaxed and carefree that she didn't get anything done.

FOOD FOR ALL YOUR NEEDS: BRAIN, BODY, BREASTS, AND BONES

Doesn't it all make sense? What's good for your female brain is good for your female body and vice versa. Why wouldn't it be that way? Your entire being is an intricate network of hormones, neurotransmitters, feedback mechanisms, and checks and balances.

For all of your female needs; brain, body, breasts, and bones, your body has guided you to an optimal eating routine that has and will continue to fulfill those needs. The **ON** Plan *is* your optimal nutrition solution for mind and body. It is not a diet or a meal plan or a set of eating rules that you must follow 100 percent of the time. It's the new, improved healthy eating guidelines for women.

•

1. No food is forbidden. All foods are acceptable when we are responding to our bodies' needs and cravings.
2. Eat a moderate amount of fat—20 to 30% of total calories.
3. Eat a high-carbohydrate diet, especially during the midday hours when your brain needs it the most.
4. Eat five small meals a day. Emphasize lunch, de-emphasize dinner, and make sure that the destabilizers (sugar, caffeine, alcohol, and artificial sweeteners) are consumed only with a small meal.
5. Eat 5 fruits and vegetables a day to provide all the nutrients and free radical–fighting antioxidants your female body needs.

and there's one more . . .

6. Hydrate your body daily.

The only female need that hasn't been addressed yet is proper hydration, so let's discuss it. Every single chemical reaction in your body takes place in a medium of water—even the reaction that releases fat from your fat cells. All of your cells need water, your muscles need water, your skin needs water, your brain needs water. **YOU NEED WATER.**
When you are dehydrated:

• You feel fatigued because your cells can't function efficiently.
• Your skin is dry, blotchy, and lacks luster.
• Your kidneys are overworked.
• Your muscles may cramp up and won't be able to keep you exercising for forty-five minutes.
• Your brain can't think straight and you get a headache.

Hydrating your body will help you to feel your best, but proper hydration goes beyond just drinking plenty of fluids.

•

You must also be aware of the hydrators and dehydrators in your diet.

Hydrators	Dehydrators
tap water	coffee
bottled water	alcohol
mineral water	soft drinks
carbonated water	juices

You've all witnessed the dehydrating effects of coffee and alcohol as the visitations to the bathroom increase shortly after consumption. For each cup of coffee you drink, you excrete two cups of fluids and put your body in negative water balance. Soft drinks and juices are so concentrated in sugar that your body can't accept them as is. They are held in your stomach while water is pulled in from your bloodstream to decrease their sugar concentration. So, initially, they dehydrate your body. You can, however, easily make juices the right concentration for your body by diluting them with an equal part of water. The same goes for the various electrolyte drinks: Dilute them with water and you are on the road to hydration.

Dilute your drinks and drink plenty of water. Water is the best way to quench your body's thirst because it is quickly absorbed and quickly directed to all of your cells. But you can't rely completely on your thirst signals for proper hydration. If you drink water just when you are thirsty, you'll consume only 50 percent of the fluids you body needs.

How much water should you drink a day? No one really knows where the universally accepted "eight glasses a day" recommendation came from. Maybe the right number is six glasses or ten glasses. Only your kidneys know for sure. That's why I recommend that my clients analyze the color of

•

their urine: If it's bright and colorful (dark amber), then they need to drink more water. If it's pale yellow, they have achieved proper hydration—and one of the important healthy eating guidelines for women.

EVE'S BLESSING

Now you know just about everything there is to know about your biological female food needs—for your body, brain, mind, and moods. You know why you crave certain foods, and most important, you know why you should trust and fulfill those food needs every day. Knowledge is empowering!

By following the **ON** Plan for the past five weeks, discovering your optimal healthy eating routine, and responding to all of your body's special food needs with confidence, pleasure, and satisfaction—you are on the path to a lifetime of weight control, mood enhancement, and health advancement!

You may have started reading this book wishing that you didn't have instinctive food needs, an appetite for sugar and fat, and the food-mood connection. But I hope that now you are thanking your lucky stars and drinking champagne (with a piece of chocolate, of course) in celebration.

As one of my clients put it, "This really *is* Eve's Blessing. It wouldn't surprise me if someday we found that the forbidden fruit was dipped in chocolate." It wouldn't surprise me either.

•

SUPPLEMENTS TO THE ON PLAN

THE ON PLAN PERSONAL EATING JOURNAL

As a complement to this book, The **ON** Plan Personal Eating Journal makes the important tool of record keeping simple, easy, and convenient. Small enough to fit into your purse or briefcase, it contains all the eating and exercise records you need to trust your food cravings, discover your optimal eating routine, enhance your mood and energy, and achieve a comfortable weight. To order this "companion to success," please send $6.00 plus $2.00 shipping and handling to:

The **ON** Plan
P.O. Box 4735
Portland, Maine 04112

•

SEMINARS AND WORKSHOPS

Debra Waterhouse is available for speaking engagements and training workshops. If your organization is interested in a presentation on "Why Women Need Chocolate," "Outsmarting the Female Fat Cell," or other nutrition topic, please send inquiries to:

Debra Waterhouse
6114 LaSalle Avenue
Box #342
Oakland, CA 94611

Would You Like to Share Your Experiences with the ON Plan?

If you would like to share your thoughts and awarenesses in food cravings, mood changes, energy level, weight control, and general well-being, please send comments to the above address.

•

Adrenaline a hormone released during stressful situations that triggers a cascade of physiological reactions called the "fight-or-flight" response. These reactions are designed to mobilize energy, increase alertness, and prevent injury.

Aerobic Exercise rhythmical, nonstop movement using the major muscle groups, the buttocks and the thighs, that results in a sustained increase in heart rate and breathing. Aerobic (meaning "with oxygen") exercises include walking, hiking, jogging, biking, rowing, swimming, stair climbing, cross-country skiing, aerobics classes, and step classes.

Anaerobic Exercise stop/start types of exercise that do *not* result in a sustained rise in heart rate or breathing. Anaerobic (meaning without oxygen) exercises include sprinting, golf, bowling, softball, and weight lifting.

Antioxidants a group of nutrients (including beta-carotene,

•

vitamin C, vitamin E, and various minerals) found primarily in fruits and vegetables that prevents the oxidation of cells, thereby neutralizing harmful free radicals. This interaction has been found to reduce the risk of heart disease and certain cancers.

Biological Food Craving a strong physiological desire for specific foods triggered by a need to balance nutrient, blood sugar, or brain chemical levels. Hunger always precedes biological food cravings, and improved nutritional status and mood are the result of fulfilling the cravings.

Biological Rhythms the daily, monthly, and yearly fluctuations in metabolism, hormones, and brain chemicals timed to increase wakefulness during the day and sleepiness at night.

Blood Sugar Destabilizers substances such as simple sugars, caffeine, alcohol, and artificial sweeteners that may cause a sharp rise and/or fall in blood sugar levels.

Chemoreceptors taste detectors located on the taste buds responsible for sending messages to the brain to determine the palatability of food.

Cholecystokinin a satiety chemical released from the stomach and intestine that gives feedback to the brain to stop eating.

Complex Carbohydrates long chains of glucose molecules that take approximately two hours to be digested and absorbed into the bloodstream and are found in starches such as breads, potatoes, rice, pasta, and cereals.

Dopamine a brain chemical released after eating high-protein foods that can increase alertness and concentration.

Emotional Food Craving a strong psychological desire for certain foods triggered by an unsatisfied emotional need. Negative mood, not physiological hunger, precedes emo-

•

tional food cravings, and an intensified negative feeling is the result of fulfilling the craving.

Endorphins a group of brain chemicals released during physical pain, exercise, pleasurable situations, or after eating chocolate and fat that reduce pain sensitivity and increase energy and positive mood.

Endorphin Surge a significant rise in a woman's brain endorphin levels during a forty-eight-hour time span around ovulation that has a positive effect on mood, energy, and sex drive.

Endorphin Withdrawal negative mood changes associated with a significant decline in brain endorphin levels.

Estrogen a female sex hormone released from the ovaries, adrenal glands, and fat cells responsible for sexual characteristics and fertility.

Female Food Craving a normal, biological need for a specific food that will balance a woman's body and mind and revitalize her well-being.

Fibrocystic Breasts benign, painful breast lumps that often intensify premenstrually.

Free Radicals unstable waste products of cellular metabolism that trigger a chain reaction of cellular damage and may increase the risk of heart disease and certain cancers.

Galanin a brain chemical stimulating fat cravings and fat storage that is usually released in the afternoon hours.

Insulin a pancreatic hormone responsible for transporting glucose molecules from the bloodstream into the cells.

Menopause a term often used interchangeably with *perimenopause* that marks the "pause" of "menses" or the last monthly menstrual cycle. Symptoms describing menopause are included in the definition of perimenopause.

Metabolism the speed at which the body uses calories for daily functioning. Metabolism can vary daily, is greatest

•

during the first twelve hours of the day, and is elevated with exercise and increased muscle mass.

Negative Calcium Balance a term used to describe poor calcium status that occurs when more calcium is excreted from the body than is consumed and deposited in the bones.

Neuropeptide Y a brain chemical stimulating carbohydrate cravings that is usually released in the early morning hours.

Neurotransmitters any brain chemical that transmits specific messages from one brain cell (also called *neuron*) to another.

Osteoporosis the premature loss of bone minerals resulting in porous, less dense bones that are more likely to fracture.

Perimenopause a term used to describe the six-month to fifteen-year transition to menopause during which estrogen levels decline causing a variety of physical and psychological changes such as weight gain, hot flashes, insomnia, depression, anxiety, forgetfulness, and intensified food cravings.

Phenylethylamine a brain chemical released when positive emotions such as falling in love are experienced. This chemical is also present in some foods including chocolate.

Phytochemicals natural disease-fighting agents found in fruits and vegetables that may help to eliminate harmful substances and reduce the risk of cancer.

Positive Calcium Balance a term used to describe healthy calcium status that occurs when more calcium is consumed and deposited in the bones than is excreted from the body.

•

Postmenopause   a term used to describe the time in a woman's life after she has stopped menstruating.

Premenopausal   a term used to describe women in their reproductive years before the transition to menopause.

Premenstrual   a term used to describe the last two weeks of each monthly menstrual cycle, from ovulation to the first day of blood flow.

Premenstrual Syndrome (PMS)   the cyclical reoccurrence of mild to moderate physical and psychological changes that begin after ovulation and intensify the few days before menses. Symptoms include depression, irritability, headaches, fluid retention, breast tenderness, and food cravings.

Saturated Fat   the type of fat that has been found to increase blood cholesterol levels and is present in all animal foods plus a few vegetable foods such as palm oil, coconuts, and coconut oil.

Seasonal Affective Disorder   the extreme negative effect of the fewer daylight hours of winter on biological rhythms, mood, and energy levels. Symptoms include depression, lethargy, low brain serotonin levels, and carbohydrate cravings.

Serotonin   a brain chemical communicating calmness and mood stability. Carbohydrates, sunlight, and certain hormones have a positive effect on brain serotonin levels.

Simple Carbohydrates   short chains of glucose molecules that are quickly digested and absorbed into the bloodstream and are found in high-sugar foods such as candy, jam, fruit, fruit juice, and soft drinks.

Stearic Acid   a unique type of saturated fat that has been found to lower blood cholesterol levels and is present in chocolate and some other foods.

•

Suprachiasmatic Nucleus a special timepiece in the brain that coordinates all bodily processes and synchronizes biological rhythms.

Testosterone a male sex hormone responsible for sexual characteristics, increased muscle mass, and libido.

Weight-Bearing Exercise any physical movement that forces the skeletal bones to carry weight (body weight or external weight) and leads to increased bone density. Weight-bearing exercises include walking, dancing, tennis, golf, gardening, house cleaning, and weight lifting.

●

REFERENCES

Albus, M. 1988. Cholecystokinin. *Prog. Neuropsychopharmacol. Biol. Psychiatry* 12:5–21.

Anderson, I.M. et al. 1990. Dieting reduces plasma tryptophan and alters brain 5-HT function in women. *Psychol. Med.* 20:785–91.

Anderson, M. et al. 1988. Premenstrual syndrome research: Using the NIMH guidelines. *J. Clin. Psychiatry* 49:484.

Arora, R.C. et al. 1984. Seasonal variations of serotonin uptake in normal controls and depressed patients. *Biol. Psychiatry* 19:795–804.

Ashby, C.R. et al. 1988. Alteration of platelet serotonergic mechanisms and monoamine oxidase activity in premenstrual syndrome. *Biol. Psychiatry* 61:1179–84.

Ashley, D.V.M. 1985. Factors affecting the selection of protein and carbohydrate from a dietary choice. *Nutr. Research* 5:555–71.

Baile, C.A. et al. 1986. Role of cholecystokinin and opioid peptides in the control of food intake. *Physiol. Rev.* 66:172–235.

Ballinger, C.B. et al. 1982. Some biochemical findings during pregnancy and after delivery in relation to mood change. *Psychol. Med.* 12:549–56.

Ballinger, C.B. et al. 1987. Hormonal profiles and psychological symptoms in perimenopausal women. *Maturitas* 9:235–51.

Ballor, D. et al. 1991. A meta-analysis of the factors affecting exercise-induced changes in body mass, fat mass, and fat-free mass in males and females. *Int. J. Obes.* 15:717–26.

•

257

Bancroft, J. et al. 1990. Blunting of neuroendocrine responses to infusion of L-tryptophan in women with premenstrual mood change. *Psychol. Med.* 21:305.

———. 1993. The impact of oral contraceptives on perimenstrual mood, clumsiness, food cravings, and other symptoms. *J. Psychosom. Res.* 37:195–202.

Banks, W.A. et al. 1988. Interactions between the blood-brain barrier and endogenous peptides: Clinical implications. *Am. J. Med. Sci.* 295:459–65.

———. 1988. Permeability of the blood-brain barrier to neuropeptides: The case for penetration. *Psychoneuroendocrinology* 10:385–99.

Berk, T. et al. 1986. Role of pyloris in mediating cholecystokinin-stimulated satiety in the Zucker Rat. *Dig. Dis. Sci.* 31:502–5.

Binkley, S. at al. 1990. Human daily rhythms measured for one year. *Physiol. Behav.* 48:293–98.

Blair, A. et al. 1990. Does emotional eating interfere with success in attempts at weight control? *Appetite* 15:151–57.

Blier, P. et al. 1990. A role for the serotonin system in the mechanism of action of antidepressent treatments. *J. Clin. Psychiatry* 5:14–20.

Block, G. et al. 1985. Nutrient sources in the American Diet: Quantitative data from the NHANES II survey. 2. Macronutrients and fat. *Am. J. Epidem.* 122:27–40.

Blum, I., et al. 1992. The influence of meal composition on plasma serotonin and norepinephrine concentrations. *Metabolism* 41:137.

———. 1993. Food preferences, body weight, and platelet-poor plasma serotonin and catecholamines. *Am. J. Clin. Nutr.* 54:486–9.

Blundell, J. E. et al. 1986. Physiological determinants of food choice and nutrient selection. *Appetite* 7:232.

———. 1986. Serotonin manipulations and the structure of feeding behavior. *Appetite* 7:39–56.

———. 1987. Serotonergic modulations and the pattern of eating and the profile of hunger-satiety in humans. *Int. J. Obes.* 11:141–55.

———. 1993. Dietary fat and the control of energy intake: Evaluating the effects of fat on meal size and post-meal satiety. *Am. J. Clin. Nutr.* 57:772s–78s.

———. 1994. Carbohydrates and human appetite. *Am. J. Clin. Nutr.* 59:728–34.

Boeder, C. et al. 1992. The effects of either high intensity resistance or endurance training on resting metabolic rate. *Am. J. Clin. Nutr.* 55:802–10.

Bonanome, A. et al. 1988. Effect of dietary stearic acid on plasma cholesterol and lipoprotein levels. *N. Eng. J. Med.* 318:1244–48.

Both-Orthman, B. et al. 1988. Menstrual cycle phase-related changes in appetite in patients with premenstrual syndrome and in control subjects. *Am. J. Psychiatry* 145:628–31.

Bowen, D.J., et al. 1990. Variations in food preference and consumption across the menstrual cycle. *Physiol. Behav.* 47:287–91.

Brinton, L. 1990. The relationship of benign breast disease to breast cancer. *Ann. NY Acad. Sci.* 586:266–71.

•

Campfield, L.A., et al. 1986. Functional coupling between transient declines in blood glucose and feeding behavior: Temporal relationships. *Brain Res. Bull.* 17:427–33.

Carpenter, K.J. 1992. Protein requirements of adults from an evolutionary perspective. *Am. J. Clin. Nutr.* 55:913–7.

Carper, J. 1993. *Food—Your Miracle Medicine.* New York: Harper Collins.

Charles, P. 1992. Calcium absorption and calcium bioavailability. *J. Int. Med.* 231:161–68.

Charney, D.S. et al. 1990. Serotonin function and human anxiety disorders. *Ann. NY Acad. Sci.* 600:558–72.

Christensen, L., et al. 1993. Effect of meal composition on mood. *Behav. Neuroscience* 2:346–53.

Christie, M.J. et al. 1982. Physical dependence on physiologically released endogenous opiates. *Life. Sci.* 30:1173–77.

Chung, Y. et al. 1989. Seasonal affective disorder: Shedding light on a dark subject. *Postgrad. Med.* 86:309–14.

Cohen, I.T. et al. 1987. Food cravings, mood and the menstrual cycle. *Hormones and Behav.* 21:457–70.

Cooper, P.J. et al. 1986. Dysphoric mood and overeating. *Br. J. Clin. Psychol.* 25:155.

Dalvit-McPhillips, S.P. 1983. The effect of the human menstrual cycle on nutrient intake. *Physiol. Behav.* 31:209–12.

De Graaf, C. et al. 1992. Short-term effects of different amounts of protein, fats, and carbohydrates on satiety. *Am. J. Clin. Nutr.* 55:33–8.

Donrich, C. et al. 1989. Postponment of satiety by blockage of CCK receptors. *Science* 1590–11.

Drewnowski, A. et al. 1983. Cream and sugar: Human preferences for high fat foods. *Physiol. Behav.* 30:629–33.

———. 1985. Sweet tooth reconsidered: Taste preferences in human obesity. *Physiol. Behav.* 35:617–22.

———. 1987. Changes in mood after carbohydrate consumption. *Am. J. Clin. Nutr.* 46:703.

———. 1987. Taste and eating disorders. *Am. J. Clin. Nutr.* 46:442–50.

———. 1989. Sensory preferences for fat and sugar in adolescence and adult life. *Ann. N.Y. Acad. Sci.* 561:243–49.

———. 1989. Sugar and fat: Sensory and hedonic evaluation of liquid and solid foods. *Physiol. Behav.* 45:177–83.

———. 1990. Fat aversion in eating disorders. *Appetite* 10:119–31.

———. 1991. Taste preferences in human obesity: Environmental and familial factors. *Am. J. Clin. Nutr.* 54:635–41.

•

259

———. 1992. Sensory properties of fat and fat replacements. *Nutr. Rev.* 50:17–20.

———. 1992. Taste respones and food preferences in obese women: Effects of weight cycling. *Int. J. Obes.* 16:639–48.

———. 1992. Taste responses and preferences for sweet high-fat foods: Evidence for opiod involvement. *Physiol. Behav.* 51:371–79.

Duester, P.A. et al. 1987. Magnesium and zinc status during the menstrual cycle. *Am. J. Obstet. Gynecol.* 157:964.

Eaton, S.B. Humans, lipids and evolution. 1992. *Lipids* 27:814–20.

Eaton, S.B., et al. 1991. Calcium in evolutionary perspective. *Am. J. Clin. Nutr.* 54:281–7.

Facchinetti, F. et al. 1987. Premenstrual fall of plasma B-endorphin in patients with premenstrual syndrome. *Fertility & Sterility.* 47:570–73.

———. 1988. Transient failure of central opiod tonus and premenstrual symptoms. *J. Reprod. Med.* 33:633–38.

Fairburn, C.G., et al. 1992. Eating habits and eating disorders during pregnancy. *Psychosom. Med.* 54:665–72.

Ferin, M. 1984. Endogenous opiod peptides and the menstrual cycle. *Trends Neurosci.* 3:194.

Fiatarone, M.A., et al. 1988. Endogenous opioids and the exercise-induced augmentation of natural killer cell activity. *J. Lab. Clin. Med.* 112:544–50.

Fischette, C.T. et al. 1984. Sex steroid modulation of the serotonin behavioral syndrome. *Life Sci.* 35:1197–1206.

Freud, S. 1938. *Totem and Taboo.* Harmondsworth, Middlesex: Penguin Books.

———. 1952. *The Case of Dora and Other Papers.* New York: W.W. Norton and Company.

———. 1961. *Civilization and Its Discontents.* New York: W.W. Norton and Company.

Gallant, M. et al. 1987. Pyridoxine and magnesium status of women with premenstrual syndrome. *Nutr. Res.* 7:243–53.

Giannini, A.J. et al. 1990. Beta-endorphin decline in late luteal phase dysphoric disorder. *Int. J. Psychiatry Med.* 20:270.

Genezzani, A.R. et al. 1981. B-lipotropin and B-endorphin in physiological and surgical menopause. *J. Endocron. Invest.* 4:475–78.

———. 1981. B-lipotropin and B-endorphin levels during pregnancy. *Clin. Endocrin.* 14:409–18.

George, C.F. et al. 1989. The effect of L-tryptophan on daytime sleep latency in normals: Correlations with blood levels. *Sleep* 12:345.

Geracioti, T.D. et al. 1988. Impaired cholecyctokinin secretion in bulimia nervosa. *N. Eng. J. Med.* 319:683–88.

Gerlo, E.A. et al. 1991. Age and sex-related differences for the urinary excretion of norepinephrine, epinephrin, and dopamine in adults. *Clin. Chem.* 37:875.

Gitlin, M.J. et al. 1989. Psychiatric syndromes linked to reproductive function in women: a review of current knowledge. *Am. J. Psychiatry* 146:1413.

•

Gladis, G.S. 1987. Premenstrual exacerbation of binge eating in bulimia. *Am. J. Psychiatry* 144:1592.

Glick, R. et al. 1991. Treatment of premenstrual dysphoric symptoms in depressed women. *JAMA.* 46:182.

Goodwin, G.M. et al. 1987. Dieting changes serotonergic function in women, not men: Implications for the aetiology of anorexia nervosa? *Psychol. Med.* 17:839–42.

Greeley, S. 1989. American women in midlife: Eating patterns and menopause. *Ann. NY Acad. Sci.* 570:162–66.

Guinan, M.E. 1988. PMS or prefollicular phase euphoria. *J. Am. Med. Wom. Assoc.* 43:91.

Haines, P. et al. 1992. Eating patterns and energy intake of U.S. women. *J. Am. Diet. Assoc.* 92:698–707.

Harris, B. et al. 1989. The hormonal environment of post-natal depression. *Br. J. Psychiat.* 154:660–67.

Hartman, E. 1986. Effect of L-tryptophan and other amino acids on sleep. *Nutr. Rev.* May.

Heaney, R. 1992. Calcium in the prevention and treatment of osteoporosis. *J. Int. Med.* 231:169–80.

Herman, C.P. et al. 1987. Anxiety, hunger and eating behaviour. *J. Abnormal. Psychol.* 96:264–69.

Hill, A.J. et al. 1986. Macronutrients and satiety: The effects of nutritional composition and food deprivation on subjective hunger, satiety, and food preference. *Nutrition and Behavior* 3:133–144.

———. 1991. Food craving, dietary restraint and mood. *Appetite* 17:187–97.

Hofeldt, F.D. 1989. Reactive hypoglycemia. *Endocrinol. Metab. Clin. North Am.* 18:185–201.

Hunter, M et al. 1986. Relationships between psychological symptoms, somatic complaints and menopausal status. *Maturitas* 8:217–28.

Hurst, W.J. et al. 1982. Biogenic amines in chocolate—A review. *Nutr. Rep. Int.* 26:1081–6.

Jacobson, J.N. 1989. Premenstrual syndrome treatments. *J. Clin. Psychiatry* 50:393.

Jenkins, D. et al. 1989. Nibbling versus gorging: Metabolic advantages of increased meal frequency. *N. Eng. J. Med.* 321:929–34.

———. 1992. Metabolic advantages of spreading the nutrient load: Effects on increased meal frequency in non-insulin dependent diabetes. *Am. J. Clin. Nutr.* 55:461–67.

Jimerson, D.C., et al. 1990. Eating disorders and depressions: Is there a serotonin connection? *Bio. Psych.* 28:443–54.

Kaplin, J.R., et al. 1991. The effects of fat and cholesterol on social behavior in monkeys. *Psychsom. Med.* 53:634–42.

Kasper, S. et al. 1989. Epidemiological findings of seasonal changes in mood and behavior. *Arch. Gen. Psychiatry* 46:823–33.

•

Kerr, D. et al. 1993. Effect of caffeine on the recognition of and responses to hypoglycemia in humans. *Ann. Intern. Med.* 119:799–804.

Knekt, P. et al. 1990. Dietary fat and risk of breast cancer. *Am. J. Clin. Nutr.* 52:903–8.

Kräuchi K. et al. 1990. The relationship of affective state to dietary preference: Winter depression and light therapy as a model. *J. Affective Disord.* 20(1):43.

Kristal, A et al. 1992. Long-term maintenance of a low-fat diet: Durability of fat related dietary habits in the Women's Health Trial. *J. Am. Diet. Assoc.* 92:553–59.

Kyrkouli, S.E. et al. 1986. Galanin: Stimulation of feeding induced by medial hypothalmic injection of this novel peptide. *Eur. J. Pharmacol.* 122:159.

Kyrkouli, S.E. et al. 1990. Stimulation of feeding by galanin: Anatomical localization and behavioral specificity of these peptides effects in the brain. *Peptides* II:1–15.

Laatikainen, T. et al. 1985. Plasma B-endorphin and the menstrual cycle. *Fertility & Sterility* 44:206.

Laessle, R.G. et al. 1990. Mood changes and physical complaints during the normal menstrual cycle in healthy young women. *Psychoneurodendocrinology* 15:131.

Laessle, R.G. et al. 1989. Behavioral and biological correlates of dietary restraint in normal life. *Appetite* 12:83–94.

Lapierre, H.R., et al. 1990. The neuropsychiatric effects of aspartame in normal volunteers. *J. Clin. Pharm.* 30:454–60.

Lappalainen, R. et al. 1990. Hunger/craving responses and reactivity to food stimuli during fasting and dieting. *Int. J. Obes.* 14:679–88.

Lawton, C.L. et al. 1992. Overeating of fat in obese women: Failure of high fat intake to suppress later food intake. *Int. J. Obes.* 16:12.

Leathwood, P. et al. 1983. Diet-induced mood changes in normal populations. *J. Psychiat. Res.* 17:147–54.

Leibowitz, S.F. et al. 1986. Brain serotonin and eating behavior. *Appetite* 7:1–14.

———. 1989. Medial hypothalamic serotonin: Role in circadian patterns of feeding and macronutrient selection. *Brain Res.* 503:132–40.

Levine, A.S. et al. 1985. Opioids and consummatory behavior. *Brain Res. Bull.* 14:633–72.

Lissner, L. et al. 1988. Variation in energy intake during the menstrual cycle: Implications for food-intake research. *Am. J. Clin. Nutr.* 48:956–62.

Longcope, C. et al. 1986. Steroid and gonadotropin levels in women during the peri-menopausal years. *Maturitas* 8:189–96.

Lubin, F. et al. 1989. Nutritional factors associated with benign breast disease etiology: A case-control study. *Am. J. Clin. Nutr.* 50:551–56.

Lurie, S. et al. 1990. The premenstrual syndrome. *Obstet. Gynecol. Surv.* 45(4):220–28.

Lydiard, R.B. et al. 1993. CSF cholecystokinen octapeptide in patients with bulimia nervosa and in normal comparison subjects. *Am. J. Psychiatry* 150:1099–1101.

•

Lyons, P.M. et al. 1988. Serotonin precursor influenced by type of carbohydrate meal in healthy adults. *Am. J. Clin. Nutr.* 47:433–39.

MacClancy, J. 1992. *Consuming Culture*. New York: Henry Holt.

McKee, L.M., et al. 1990. Genetic and environmental origins of food patterns. *Nutr. Today* Sept.

McKinlay, J. et al. 1986. The relative contributions of endocrine changes and social circumstances to depression in mid-aged women. *J. Health. Soc. Behav.* 28:345–56.

Manocha, S. et al. 1986. A study of dietary intake in pre- and post-menstrual period. *Hum. Nutr. Appl. Nutr.* 40A:213–6.

Marano, H.E. 1993. Chemistry and craving. *Psych. Today* Jan.

Margen, S. and the editors of the University of California at Berkeley Wellness Letter. 1992. *The Wellness Encyclopedia of Food and Nutrition*. New York: Rebus.

Mascio, P. et al. 1991. Antioxidant defense systems: The role of carotenoids, tocopherols, and thiols. *Am. J. Clin. Nutr.* 53:194–200.

Maurizi, C.P. 1990. The therapeutic potential for tryptophan and melatonin: Possible roles in depression, sleep, Alzheimer's disease and abnormal aging. *Med. Hypotheses* 31:233.

Mattes, R.D. 1990. Effects of aspartame and sucrose on hunger and energy intake in humans. *Physiol. Behav.* 47:1037–44.

Mattes, R.D., et al. 1988. The chemical senses and nutrition. *Nutr. Today* May.

Michell, G.F. et al. 1989. Effect of bupropion on chocolate craving. *Am. J. Psychiatry* 146:119.

Monneuse, M.O. et al. 1991. Impact of sex and age on sensory evaluation of sugar and fat in dairy products. *Physiol. Behav.* 50:1111–17.

Moller, S.E. 1985. Tryptophan to competing amino acids in depressive disorder: Relation to efficacy of antidepressive treatments. *Acta. Psychiat. Scand. Suppl.* 325:3.

Morley, J.E. et al. 1982. The role of endogenous opiates as regulators of appetite. *Am. J. Clin. Nutr.* 35:757–61.

———. 1987. Effect of neuropeptide Y on ingestive behaviors in the rat. *Am. J. Physiol.* 252:R599–609.

Mortola, J.F. et al. 1989. Depressive episodes in premenstrual syndrome. *Am. J. Obstet. & Gynecol.* 161:1682–7.

Murphy, B.P.E. 1991. General review: Steroids and depression. *J. Steroid Biochem. Mol. Biol.* 38:537–39.

National Research Counci, Food and Nutrition Board. 1989. *Recommended Dietary Allowances*, 10th edition. Washington, DC: National Academy Press.

Norton, P. et al. 1993. Physiologic control of food intake by neural and chemical mechanisms. *JADA.* 93(4):450–54.

O'Connor, P.J. et al. 1992. Psychobiologic responses to exercise at different times of the day. *Med. Sci. Sports Exerc.* 24:714–9.

Odink, J. et al. 1990. Circadian and circatrigintan rhythms of biogenic amines in premenstrual syndrome. *Psychosom. Med.* 52:346.

•

Okano, T. et al. 1990. Endocrine studies of the maternity blues. *Clin. Neuropharmac.* 13:532.

Pennington, J.A.T. and H. N. Church. 1985. *Food Values of Portions Commonly Used.* 14th ed. Philadelphia: J.B. Lippincott Co.

Peterkin, B. 1986. Women's diets: 1977 and 1985. *J. Nutr. Educ.* 18:251–257.

Pliner, P. et al. 1983. Food intake, body weight, and sweetness preferences over the menstrual cycle in humans. *Physiol. Behav.* 30:663–666.

Popkin, B.M., et al. 1989. Food consumption trends of U.S. women: Patterns and determinants between 1971 and 1985. *Am. J. Clin. Nutr.* 49:1307–19.

Prewitt, T. et al. 1991. Changes in body weight, body composition, and energy intake in women fed high- and low-fat diets. *Am. J. Clin. Nutr.* 54:304–10.

Price, W.A. et al. 1986. Serotonin Syndrome: A case report. *J. Clin. Pharmacol.* 26:77.

Prior, J.C. et al. 1987. Conditioning exercise decreases premenstrual symptoms: A prospective, controlled 6-month trial. *Fertility & Sterility* 47:402.

Pyror, W. 1991. The antioxidant nutrients and disease prevention: What do we know and what do we need to find out? *Am. J. Clin. Nutr.* 53:391s.

Raben, A. et al. 1994. Increased postprandial thermogenesis after simple compared with complex carbohydrates in two carbohydrate-rich isoenergetic meals. *Am. J. Clin. Nutr.* 59:789.

Ramirez, I. 1990. Why does sugar taste good? *Neurosci. Biobehav. Rev.* 14:125–34.

Rapkin, A.J. et al. 1987. Whole-blood serotonin in premenstrual syndrome. *Obstet. Gynecol.* 70:533–37.

———. 1990. Tryptophan and neutral amino acids in premenstrual syndrome. *Am. J. Psychiatry* 147:1634–36.

Rivera-Tovar, A.D. et al. 1990. Late luteal phase dysphoric disorder in young women. *Am. J. Psychiat.* 147:1634.

Rodin, J. 1991. Effect of pure sugars vs. mixed starch fructose loads on food intake. *Appetite* 17:213–19.

Rodin, J. et al. 1990. Do food cravings exist and why? Repeated measures of food cravings in healthy women. *Appetite* 17:177–85.

———. 1991. Food cravings in relation to body mass index, restraint and estradiol levels. *Appetite* 17:177–85.

Rogers, P.J. et al. 1989. Separating the actions of sweetness and calories: Effects of saccharin and carbohydrates on hunger and food intake in human subjects. *Physiol. Behav.* 45: 1093–9.

Rolls, B.J. 1986. Sensory-specific satiety. *Nutr. Rev.* 44:93–101.

Rozin, P., et al. 1991. Chocolate craving and liking. *Appetite* 17:199–212.

Rubinow, D.R. et al. 1984. Prospective assessment of menstrually related mood disorders. *Am. J. Psychiatry* 141:684–86.

———. 1986. Changes in plasma hormones across the menstrual cycle in patients with menstrually-related mood disorder and in control subjects. *Am. J. Obstet. & Gynecol.* 158:5.

———. 1986. Premenstrual mood changes: Characteristic patterns in women with and without premenstrual syndrome. *J. Affective. Disord.* 10:85.

•

———. 1987. Mood disorders and the menstrual cycle. *J. Reprod. Med.* 32:389–94.

Schapira, D. 1991. Diet, obesity, fat distribution and cancer in women. *J. Am. Med. Wom. Assoc.* 46:126–31.

Schmidt, P.J. et al. 1991. Lack of effect of induced menses on symptoms in women with premenstrual syndrome. *N. Engl. J. Med.* 324:1174.

Schuman, M. et al. 1987. Sweets, chocolate, and atypical depressive traits. *J. of Nervous and Mental Disease* 178(8):491–95.

Severino, S.K. et al. 1989. Spectral analysis of cyclic symptoms in late luteal phase dysphoric disorder. *Am. J. Psychiatry* 146:155.

Shor-Posner, G. et al. 1986. Hypothalmic serotonin in the control of meal patterns and micronutrient selection. *Brain Res. Bull.* 17:633–71.

Smith, J.R. et al. 1991. Fat and satiety: Comparison of the suppressive effect of fat and carbohydrate supplements on energy and nutrient intakes in humans. *Int. J. Obes.* 15:11.

Smith, S. et al. 1969. Food cravings, depression, and premenstrual problems. *Psychosom. Med.* 31:381.

Spring, B. 1989. Psychobiological effects of carbohydrates. *J. Clin. Psychiatry* 50:27–33.

Spring, B. et al. 1987. Carbohydrates, tryptophan and behavior. *Psychol. Bull.* 102:234–56.

Stallone, D. et al. 1989. Cholecyctokinin-induced anorexia depends on serotoninergic function. *Am. J. Physiol.* 256:1138–41.

Stellman, S. et al. 1986. Short report: Artificial sweetener use and one-year weight changes among women. *Prev. Med.* 15:195–202.

Stephan, A.M. et al. 1990. Trends in individual consumption of dietary fat in the United States, 1920–1984. *Am. J. Clin. Nutr.* 52:457–69.

Stone, A.B. et al. 1991 Fluoxetine in the treatment of late luteal phase dysphoric disorder. *J. Clin. Psychiatry* 52:290.

Straten, M. 1991. The effect of exercise on food intake in men and women. *Am. J. Clin. Nutr.* 53:27–31.

Tam, W.K.Y. 1985. The menstrual cycle and platelet 5-HT uptake. *Psychosom. Med.* 47:352–62.

Taylor, D.L. et al. 1984. Serotonin levels and platelet uptake during premenstrual tension. *Neuropsychobiology* 12:16–18.

Thoren, P. et al. 1990. Endorphins and exercise: Physiological mechanisms and clinical applications. *Med. Sci. Sports Exercise* 22:417–425.

Tilyard, M.W. et al. 1992. Treatment of postmenopausal osteoporosis with calcitrol or calcium. *N. Engl. J. Med.* 326:357.

Tomelleri, R et al. 1987. Menstrual cycle and food cravings in young college women. *J. Am. Diet. Assoc.* 87:311–15.

Tuschi, R.J. 1990. From dietary restraint to binge eating: Some theoretical considerations. *Appetite* 14:105–9.

U.S. Dept. of Health & Human Services. 1989. Nutrition monitoring in the U.S. Publication no. (PHS) 89–1255.

•

Veith, J.L. et al. 1984. Plasma B-endorphin, pain thresholds and anxiety levels across the human menstrual cycle. *Physiol. Behav.* 32:31.

Walden, T. et al. 1990. Long-term effects of dieting on resting metabolic rate in obese outpatients. *J. Am. Med. Assoc.* 264:707–11.

Wardle, J. 1987. Hunger and satiety: A multidimensional assessment of responses to caloric loads. *Physiology and Behavior* 40:577–82.

Warner, P. et al. 1991. The relationship between perimenstrual depressive mood and depressive illness. *J. Affect. Disord.* 23:9.

Weil, A.J.; and W. Rosen. 1983. *Chocolate to Morphine.* New York: Houghton Mifflin.

Weingarten, H.P. 1991. Cravings for food: Four new studies. *Appetite* 17:165.

Weingarten, H.P., et al. 1990. The phenomenology of food cravings. *Appetite* 15:231–46.

——. 1991. Food cravings in a college population. *Appetite* 17:167–75.

Whybrow, P. and R. Bahr. 1988. *The Hibernation Response.* New York: Avon Books.

Wing, R. 1992. Weight cycling in humans: A review of the literature. *Ann. Behav. Med.* 14:113–19.

Wurtman, J.J. 1985. Neurotransmitter control of carbohydrate consumption. *Ann. NY Acad. Sci.* 443:145–51.

——. 1986. *Managing Your Mind and Mood through Food.* New York: Harper and Row.

——. 1989. Carbohydrates and depression. *Sci. Am. Jan.* 68–75.

Wurtman, J.J. et al. 1981. Carbohydrate craving in obese people: Suppression by treatments affecting serotoninergic transmission. *Int. J. Eating Disorders.* 1:2–11.

Wurtman, R. 1983. Neurochemical changes following high-dose aspartame with dietary carbohydrates. *N. Eng. J. Med.* 389:429.

Yogoshi, H., et al. 1986. Meal composition and plasma amino acid ratios: Effect of various proteins concentrations. *Metabolism* 9:837–42.

Yuk, V. et al. 1991. Frequency and severity of premenstrual symptoms in women taking birth control pills. *Gynecol. Obstet. Invest.* 31:42.

•

INDEX

Abstinence or denial, 6, 10, 34,
    36–37, 40–42, 72, 136
Adrenaline, 192, 251
Aerobic exercise, 217–18, 224–25,
    235, 251
Afternoon slump, 181–85
Afternoon snack, 147–48, 181–84
Alcohol, 131, 158, 168
    and calcium, 232, 233
    as dehydrator, 247
    as destabilizer, 155–56
Amines, 38
Amino acids, 114
Anaerobic exercises, 218, 251
Antioxidants, 241–43, 246, 251–52
Artificial sweeteners, 135–37,
    156–58, 168, 213, 246

Balanced meals, 43–45, 138, 150–51
Beta-carotene, 76, 241, 243
Binge Food Bellow, 70–71
Binges, 6, 37, 42, 68–71, 213
Biological food cravings
    for chocolate, 20–23
    defined, 252
    identifying, 10–11, 81–86, 88
    satisfying, 140–41

Biorhythms, 174–90, 195, 252
Blood-brain barrier, 135
Blood glucose (sugar) levels, 5, 6, 15,
    35
    and biorhythms, 174, 176, 179,
        185–87
    and destabilizers, 155–61, 169,
        252
    and food-mood competition,
        139–40
    and menopause, 187
    and postabsorptive effects, 134
    and starch, 94, 96, 98
    and stress, 192–93
    and sugar, 99–100, 102
    and timing of eating, 148–51
Bloodstream satisfaction, 127
Brain chemicals, 5, 7, 15–19
    and biorhythms, 174, 176, 179,
        181–82, 187–90
    and blood sugar levels, 150
    and chocolate, 20–21, 109–13, 182
    and dieting, 42–43
    and exercise, 209
    and fat, 39
    and healthy diet, 35
    and hunger signals, 82

●

267

Brain chemicals *(cont'd)*
    and menopause, 30
    and menstrual cycle, 24–27
    optimal eating for, 173, 190–98
    and overeating, 140–42, 180–81
    and protein, 113–14
    and satisfaction, 127, 133–37
    and starches, 94–99
    and strain, 190–98
    and sugar, 100
    and survival, 18
    and timing of eating, 148–52,
        163–65, 168
    and water, 246
Breakfast, 175–78
Breast cancer, 230, 236–44
Breast-feeding, 15, 39, 106, 244
Bulimia, 11, 133, 134
B vitamins, 76

Caffeine, 21, 37, 168, 191, 196
    amount in drinks, 158–61
    and calcium, 232
    as destabilizer, 155, 246
Calcium, 76, 120, 198, 231–35, 254
Calories
    in carbohydrates, 189–90
    in chocolate, 37
    and daily rhythms, 175, 182
    in fat, 104
Cancer, 160, 210, 228–29
"Can't stop eating" fear, 67–71, 100
Carbohydrates, 15, 16
    amount needed, 46, 47, 246
    and biorhythms, 175–77, 179–80,
        187–90
    complex, 93, 252 *(see also* Starches)
    and food-mood competition,
        138–40
    simple, 99, 255 *(see also* Sugar)
Carob, 137
Chemoreceptors, 128–31, 156, 252
Chewing, 128–29, 131–32
Childbirth, 210–11
"Chocoholic," 70
Chocolate
    afternoon urge, 182
    and brain, 15–17, 20–22
    caffeine in, 160, 161

and culture, 45
and Deprivation Wail, 68
and exercise, 212, 213
female craving for, 4, 6–7, 18–23
as "forbidden" food, 36–38
as fruit, 243
and guilt, 51
and health, 229–31
and men and women, 31–32
and menopause, 27–31
and menstrual cycle, 25–27, 185
as pleasure food, 109–13, 122
substitutes, 137
Cholecystokinin (CCK), 133–36,
    252
Cholesterol, 37, 237–38, 255
Clotting factors, 193
Coffee, 131, 158–61, 232–33, 247

Daily rhythms, 174–84
Dalton, Dr. Katrina, 23
Dehydration, 246, 247
Depression, 5, 10, 28, 38, 50, 84, 86,
    110, 152, 189
Deprivation Wail, 68
Destabilizers, 155–61, 168, 246, 252
Diabetes, 38, 210, 228
Dieting, 5, 35, 42–43, 48, 57, 72–73,
    158
Digestion, 139
Dinner, 44, 45, 162–68, 177,
    184–85, 246
Diuretics, natural, 118
Dopamine, 113–14, 179, 252

Eating
    "around the craving," 73–74, 137
    optimal routine, 55–57, 174–84
    pleasure, 50–53
    rules of society, 34–47
    for satisfaction, 126–46
    See also **ON** plan
Electrolytes, 117, 247
Emotional food craving, 10–11,
    81–86, 252–53
Emotional Outcry, 70
Empowerment Eating, 14, 30, 120,
    227–48
Empty Stomach Scream, 68–69

•

Endorphins, 6, 39, 104, 162, 184
    and chocolate, 110
    defined, 16–18, 253
    and exercise, 58, 206, 210–16, 223
    releasers, 244–45
    surge, 25–27, 29, 253
Enzymes, 93, 99, 132
Essential fatty acids, 104
Estrogen, 5, 6, 7, 15, 32
    and blood sugar, 150
    defined, 253
    and dopamine, 114
    and mood swings, 24, 28–30
    and salt, 117
    and sleep, 195–96
Eve's Blessing, 32–33, 248
Exercise, 96, 149, 166, 182
    fat-burning guidelines, 217–22
    ON Plan, 58, 206–26
    and osteoporosis, 234–35
    and water, 118, 246

Fat
    balancing, 58, 238, 246
    and biorhythms, 180, 182–87
    competition, 139–40, 143
    content of foods, 80, 238–41
    and exercise, 209, 212–13, 215–22,
        224
    food converted to, 79, 153
    as "forbidden" food, 36, 39
    and health, 237–38
    and menopause, 28, 29
    and menstrual cycle, 25
    and mood, 6, 15–17
    as pleasure food, 104–9, 113, 122
    saturated, 255
    storage, 153, 182
    substitutes, 135–37, 213
    women's need for, 39, 46, 47
Fat cells, 39, 141
    and exercise, 207–9, 216–17,
        220–21
    happy, 104, 106–7
    and timing of eating, 153, 164–66
Fatigue, 50, 86, 150, 152, 188, 193,
        213, 246
Female food cravings, 86, 191
    chocolate as, 19–23

defined, 13–33, 253
    and healthy diet, 35–47
    importance of fulfilling, 13–14, 17
    trusting, 54, 66–90
Female pleasure foods, 54, 91–125
    amounts needed, 40
    chocolate as, 109–13
    fats as, 104–9
    identifying, 91–92
    protein as, 113–15
    salt as, 119–20
    starches as, 96–99
    sugars as, 102–4
    top ten list, 120–22
Fibrocystic breasts, 160, 237, 253
Fifteen-minute test, 85
Fight-or-flight response, 192
First three bites, 129–32, 134
Five fruits and vegetables a day,
        238–43, 246
Five small meals per day, 44, 47, 58,
        168, 173, 179, 187, 191, 196,
        213, 246
    as optimal routine, 149–61
Follicle-stimulating hormone, 29
Food cravings
    biological vs. emotional, 10–11,
        81–86
    and biorhythms, 23, 185–87
    combination cravings, 118–19
    common fears about, 67–81
    defined, 4, 13–33
    and exercise, 209, 212–13, 215
    and female biology, 3–8
    fulfilling, 6, 7, 11–14, 53, 74–75
    hours to say yes to, 23, 148,
        161–62, 179, 185–86
    listing, 76
    of men, 7, 8, 31–32
    and menstrual cycle, 23–27
    and ON Plan, 34, 47, 58
    and overeating, 140–42
    and sleep, 196
    and stress, 193
    and weight gain, 72–75
    See also Biological food cravings;
        Emotional food cravings;
        Female food cravings; and
        specific food types

•

Food-mood competition, 137–40, 169, 176
Food Race Roar, 69
Forbidden foods, 36–40, 246
Free radicals, 241–42, 246, 253
Fruit, 241–43, 186, 187

Galanin, 182, 184, 238, 253
Glycemic index of foods, 102
Glycogen or glucose stores, 96, 153, 175–76

Headaches, 38, 150
Health goals, 228–30
Healthy diet, 76–81
Heart disease, 160, 210, 228–30, 236–44
Hibernation Response, 189
Hormone-replacement therapy, 30, 117, 187
Hormones, 17, 28–29, 35, 92, 98, 150, 245
   and biorhythms, 174–75, 184–87
Hot flashes, 28
Hunger, 68–69, 81–84, 177–78
   /Fullness Rating Scale, 83–84, 88, 122, 143, 144
Hydrating body, 246–48
Hypoglycemia, 38, 150

Insomnia, 197–98
Insulin, 94, 150, 156–57, 253
Iron, 76, 114–15

LSD (Long Slow Distance) exercise, 210–15, 216
Lunch, 44–45, 47, 58, 166, 168, 173, 179–81, 246
Luteinizing hormone, 29

Magnesium, 21, 76
Meat, 7, 31–32, 76, 114–15
Memory loss, 28
Men
   and chocolate, 110
   cravings, 7, 8, 15, 31–32, 113
   and exercise, 220–21
   monthly changes, 30–31

Menopause, 5, 6, 14, 27–31, 50, 186, 231, 253
   and biorhythms, 188, 189
   and food cravings, 92, 186–87
   male, 30–31
   and sleep, 195
   and timing of eating, 149, 151, 167
Menstrual cycle, 23–27, 92, 184–87
Metabolism, 163, 165, 166, 253–54
   and biorhythms, 174–75, 182, 184–85
   and exercise, 208, 209, 221
Midmorning snack, 178–79
Milk products, 76, 120, 198, 231, 233, 239
Mood(s), 4, 50, 230
   and balanced meals, 43–45
   and biorhythms, 184–90
   and brain chemistry, 16
   and carbohydrates, 232
   and chocolate, 21
   enhancers, 244–45
   and exercise, 206–15
   and food cravings, 5–7, 14, 15, 18, 84–85
   and lunch, 179
   maximizing, 54–55
   and menstrual cycle, 23–27
   and menopause, 29, 30
   and salt, 115–17
   and satisfaction, 137–40
   Scale, 85, 88, 123, 143
   and starches, 93–96
   and stress, 193, 194
   and sugar, 100
   and supplements, 244
   and timing of eating, 147–71
"Morning Experiment," 71
Muscles, 7, 32, 153, 221, 246

Naps, 197
Neuropeptide Y, 176, 177, 254
Neurotransmitters, 15–16, 245, 254
Night sweats, 196, 197
Nighttime eating, 162, 166–67

OFF Plan (Outsmart Female Fat), 57, 58

•

Olfactory satisfaction, 127, 129
ON plan (**O**ptimal **N**utrition for
    Mind and Body)
    benefits of, 9, 11–12, 49–50
    and biorhythms, 174–90
    defined, 9–12, 48–65
    eating rules, 47
    evaluation, 199–205
    Exercise Plan, 206–26, 234–35
    five steps of, 9, 53–57
    and health, 227–48
    Personal Eating Journal, 249
    questionnaires on, 60–65
    seminars and workshops, 250
    Step 1, Trust Your Female Food
        Cravings, 9, 54, 60, 66–90, 200
    Step 2, Discover Your Female
        Pleasure Foods, 9, 54, 61,
        91–125, 201
    Step 3, Learn How to Eat for
        Maximum Satisfaction, 9, 54,
        62, 126–46, 202
    Step 4, Distribute Your Food to
        Maximize Mood, 9, 54–55, 63,
        147–71, 203
    Step 5, Follow Your Optimal
        Eating Routine, 9, 55, 64,
        172–205
Oral contraceptives, 117
Osteoporosis, 30, 160, 230–35, 254
Outsmarting the Female Fat Cell, 3,
    57
Overeating, 11, 79, 140–42, 180–81
Ovulation, 25–27, 29
Oxidation, 241–42

Perimenopause, 27–29, 186–87, 209,
    253, 254
Phenylethylamine, 21, 22, 137, 254
Phosphorous, 232
Phytochemicals, 242, 254
Pica cravings, 76
PMS (premenstrual syndrome), 42,
    50, 149, 151, 167, 230
    and biorhythms, 185–86, 188–89
    and chocolate, 110
    defined, 23–27, 255
    and exercise, 209
    and sleep, 195

Postabsorptive effect, 134, 137
Postmenopause, 255
Potassium, 51, 77
Pregnancy, 6, 15, 39, 76, 106, 117,
    131, 151–52
Premenstrual period
    defined, 255
    and food cravings, 5, 6, 14, 23–27,
        117, 185–86
Pre-Testosterone Syndrome, 30
Progressive relaxation, 198, 244
Protein, 122
    and biorhythms, 176, 179, 180
    and calcium loss, 231–32
    competition, 138–40, 143, 176
    and fat content, 240
    and menopause, 186, 187
    needs, 7, 31, 32, 47
    as pleasure food, 113–16

Salt, 76
    and calcium, 233
    as pleasure food, 115–20, 122
    and taste buds, 131
Satisfaction, 173
    eating for, 52–54, 126–46
    and overeating, 140–42
    Scale, 144
Seasonal Affective Disorder, 11, 188,
    189, 255
Seasons, 17, 184, 187–90
Serotonin, 5–6, 18, 114, 162
    and biorhythms, 179–80, 187–89
    and chocolate, 21, 110
    defined, 16, 255
    and dieting, 43
    and food-mood competition,
        138–40, 180
    and menopause, 28–29
    and menstrual cycle, 24–25
    releasers, 244–45
    and sleep, 195–96, 197, 198
    and starch, 93, 95
    and sugar, 98, 102, 136
Sex, 21, 26, 28, 111, 244
    as exercise, 222
Sing test, 218–20
Sleep, 5, 17, 166, 173, 195–98, 209,
    213, 214

•

Snacking, 44, 47, 147–48, 173
Soft drinks, 160–61, 232–33, 247
    diet, 158
Starch
    benefits of, 40, 46
    and biorhythms, 178, 182–83
    and brain, 92–99, 113
    cravings, 15, 16, 96–98, 122
    and exercise, 209
    and fat, 239
    and food-mood competition,
        138–39
    "forbidden," 36, 39–40
    and mood, 5–6, 91
    and sleep, 196
    and sugar, 100–2
    and women, 7
Starvation response, 106, 107, 149,
    208. See also Survival
    mechanism
Starving Children Broadcast, 69–70
Stearic acid, 37, 255
Stomach, 82, 127, 132–35
    receptors, 133, 135
Stress, 17, 149, 151–52, 173,
    188
    eating for, 191–95, 230
    and exercise, 209, 213
Sugar
    and afternoon slump, 182–83
    and brain chemistry, 16
    as destabilizer, 155, 246
    and exercise, 209, 212–13
    and fat combination cravings, 6–7,
        17, 18, 23, 32
    and fat content, 240
    as "forbidden" food, 36, 38–39
    and menopause, 28, 186–87
    and menstrual cycle, 24, 185
    and mood, 5–6, 15, 91
    as pleasure food, 98–104, 113,
        122
    and sleep, 196
    and stress, 191, 193
    substitutes, 136
    and taste buds, 130, 131
Suprachiasmatic Nucleus, 174, 256
Survival mechanism, 18, 35, 39,
    42–43, 130, 182

Target heart rate, 218–19
Taste buds, 127–32, 135
10 A.M. to 4 P.M. food cravings,
    161–62, 185–86
Testosterone, 7, 30–31, 32, 113,
    187, 256
Theobromine, 21, 137
Tofu, 79–80
Tooth decay, 37–38

Urine, 248

Vegetables, 47, 120, 180, 184, 209,
    213, 241–43
    and fat content, 239
    and menopause, 186, 187
Visual satisfaction, 127
Vitamin A, 241
Vitamin C, 15, 76, 241, 243
Vitamin supplements, 243–44

Walking, 216, 224–25, 234
Water, 118, 120, 246–48
    retention, 117–18
Weight-bearing exercise, 234–35,
    256
Weight control, 4, 7, 10, 50, 230
    and eating time, 149, 152–54
    and exercise, 215–22
    and ON Plan, 57, 58
Weight gain, 5, 43, 106
    and five meals a day, 152–53
    and food cravings, 72–75
    and menopause, 28, 29–30
    and yearly rhythms, 189–90
Weight-training, 221
White chocolate, 137
Women
    and biology of food cravings,
        15–19, 46–47
    and chocolate, 19–20, 110–11
    and endorphins, 210–11
    and exercise, 206–11
    and food and mood, 5–8
    power lunch for, 180
    See also Female food cravings;
        Female pleasure foods

Yearly rhythms, 184–85, 187–90

•